Falling from H
Martina Wol

Martina Woknitz

Falling from Heaven

A Child's Memoir of Abuse and Survival

DeBehr

Copyright by: Martina Woknitz
Publisher: Verlag DeBehr, Radeberg
English First edition: 2025
ISBN: 9783987273575
Cover graphic created via Midjourney.com

All names of people and places of action have been changed.
Equality is due to pure chance.

Why?

I keep asking myself why there are parents who can't show their children any love at all.
Why are there people who abuse children?
Why are there parents who are violent?

Children are so precious, they deserve love and care, but unfortunately the exact opposite happens time and time again.

This is what happens to Cecilia and later, unfortunately, to her little sister.

I would like to take you into the lives of the two children. This story has left me stunned and infinitely sad.

Martina Woknitz

Cecilia

My first years as a child were very nice. Until I was five years old, I lived with my grandparents in the country in a beautiful house with a great garden. My grandpa had even built me a swing. They were my mother's parents. The home-baked cakes and tasty meals were wonderful. The whole house was filled with delicious smells every day. My mouth was always watering.
Why did I live there?
Grandma told me that when I was born, my mother was still very young and far too immature for a baby. For this reason, she and mom decided that I should live with grandma and grandpa for the first few years, and as soon as my mother found an apprenticeship or a job, she would bring me to live with her. I didn't and still don't know my biological father. As a small child, I didn't think about it, I felt far too comfortable for that. I was fine, I wanted for nothing. My grandpa romped around with me in the garden, played with me in the sandpit he had built for me and showed me around with lots of explanations about nature. It was never boring, he explained everything so interestingly that I listened attentively to his words. It never occurred to me that I should return to my mother at some point. My grandma always made sure that I was clean and had nice clothes. I went to the kindergarten in the village until lunchtime. I liked it so much, I played with lots of other children and my favorite thing was painting and kneading. At home I had everything I needed for this, coloring books, drawing pads, pencils, plasticine in all variations (ice cream maker, pizza maker,

even a dentist game made of plasticine). But I also had enough of other games. Dolls in all sizes, Barbies, a doll's pram, everything that makes a child's heart happy.

When my grandma baked cakes, I was always allowed to lick out the bowl. I was covered in batter up to my ears and Grandma would laugh at me: "Angel, now go and wash up," she would laugh at such times. Yes, I was a very happy child. When I brought home something I had made myself from kindergarten, she would beam at me and praise me, immediately calling my grandpa: "Look what Cecilia has made for us."

He stroked my head: "You did a great job, sweetie." Grandma and Grandpa kept everything of mine carefully. Praise was the greatest gift for me.

When one of them had a birthday, I was always allowed to go with them to buy a present. It was the same at Christmas. But I was always so excited that I once revealed what Grandma had given me. But she wasn't angry with me. My grandparents laughed.

Of course, my mother came to visit me from time to time. However, these meetings didn't happen very often. But as I felt so comfortable, I didn't really care. I didn't have any real connection with my mother. When she came, she was usually in a bad mood, she didn't talk to me much and never brought me a small present. I don't mean presents on a grand scale, for God's sake, no. But a bar of chocolate, a surprise egg or a coloring book weren't expensive, and a small child would be happy about them. But she wasn't. When I was little, I wondered why she didn't even bring me a chocolate bar, but only in passing. I didn't really think about it.

Every evening, my grandma or grandpa would read me a story and so I slipped happily and contentedly into dreamland.

Unfortunately, I started hearing more and more conversations about how I should come back to my mother. I was still small, but I was already aware of that much. My mother was like a stranger to me. She didn't cuddle me, didn't play with me and didn't do anything else that could connect us. 'Oh nonsense, they were probably just talking. She wouldn't take me in because I was doing so well here. Nevertheless, I couldn't get the thought out of my head.

'Will I stay here forever? Oh please, please, I never want to leave here again. It's good like this. Mom comes to visit me, otherwise I live with grandma and grandpa and that's so nice.' That was all I needed. Nevertheless, I often wondered why Mom was always so serious.

I loved my grandparents so much and knew nothing else. I didn't want to give up my friends at kindergarten. No, I wanted to stay here forever and decided not to give it another thought. Everything is fine the way it is, why should it be changed?

One evening I asked this question anxiously at dinner: "Grandma ... do I have to leave you?"

Startled, she looked at me: "Why would you ask that, little mouse?" Shrugging my shoulders, I sat at the table, unable to explain it coherently: "What if my mom just takes me with her?"

With a serious expression, she pulled me onto her lap and held me tightly in her arms.

"Oh angel, you can't stay here forever. Mommy will want

to take you home one day. After all, you're her child and she loves you. Look, Grandma and Grandpa are getting older and when you have to go to school, it will be better for you to be with Mom."

"Don't you love me anymore?" I asked hesitantly.

"But of course, we love you more than anything, you mustn't forget that. But children also belong with their parents, in your case with your mom."

"I'm very sweet, Grandma. I'll always help you when I'm a bit bigger. Please, let me stay with you," I begged with tears in my eyes.

"Little mouse, it's not that far yet. Who knows how everything will turn out. Do we want to drive ourselves crazy already? You're still here and that's as far as we think for now, okay? Would you like another hot chocolate? And another story?"

Grandma wanted to distract me and I pretended that she had done it. But I never let go of that thought. Not for a single day. I was just sad and hoped that the day Mum came to get me would never come and that she didn't want me with her. Maybe that was actually the case. She didn't want me at all and just left me here. This thought comforted me a little.

My grandpa or grandma took me to kindergarten every day and picked me up again at lunchtime. The whole way home, I babbled away and told them everything I had experienced and done. I was always sweet, but very talkative and a bit wild. Romping and chattering was what I did best. When I think about it today, I ask myself, where has this happy child gone? The answer is quite clear - with grandma and grandpa. That's where I left my carefree and happy childhood.

That day, my grandpa picked me up from kindergarten. I ran into his arms and he cuddled me as usual. On the way home, he told me: "Your mom is with us."
I nodded my head. It was still nothing special for me. My grandpa was very quiet on the way home, but I chattered and chattered. When I got home, I heard the two women arguing.
"Why don't you leave Cecilia here? She's so happy."
"Yes, but I want her to come and visit me. We'll see if she might even want to come to me." I understood these words perfectly, raced into the kitchen, threw myself into Grandma's arms and screamed: "No, I don't want to leave here, I want to stay here."
Mom approached me cautiously: "Cecilia, I just want to take you for a visit. Look, I've met a man who's very nice and would like to meet you too."
I didn't understand anything, nothing at all. There was only one thing I knew for sure - I never wanted to leave the most beautiful place in the world and my dearest grandparents.
"No!" I screamed.
"Yes, you do!" Mum barked right back and I flinched in shock. "You belong to me now. The fact that you lived here was an emergency solution, but now you should be with me, I'm your mom."
She didn't give me a hug or try to explain everything to me calmly. It was more like she decided and I had to comply. That was that. It certainly didn't occur to her that she wanted to tear me out of everything.
That day, she took me home with her for the whole

afternoon. I reluctantly went with her, of course. I had no other choice. We had to take the train into town, then it was just a short walk and we were there. A huge block of flats stood in front of me, with these huge squares all around. Building after building. I'd never seen anything like it. Heavens, how many people live here? On the third floor, Mom unlocked a door and pushed me inside. It smelled funny here, I couldn't describe the smell. Somehow old and musty, not like Grandma's, like fresh laundry and cake, clean and delicious. When I was pushed into the living room, I saw what else it smelled like - cigarette smoke. My mom's boyfriend was sitting in an armchair smoking. He was holding a bottle in his hand.

"Cecilia, this is Jens, my boyfriend. He lives here with me ... say hello!"

"Good afternoon," I whispered.

Jens stood up and approached me with a smile: "You're a pretty girl with such a nice name." He was actually quite nice, but I wanted to get back to Grandma. Hopefully the afternoon would be over soon. My mother showed me around the apartment and then my room. I was so shocked I couldn't get a word out. My 'realm' was no bigger than Grandma's storage room and there wasn't a bed in it either. There was just a mattress on the floor with sheets, pillows and a blanket.

"We'll buy a bed for you," Mom replied to my shocked face. Suddenly, tears welled up in my eyes: "I want to go to my grandma," I cried.

Comfort me? Not a chance. Mom imitated me and immediately snapped at me: "That's all right now. I'll take you to your beloved grandma later. But I'll tell you one thing: your days with them are numbered. As soon as everything is sorted out, you'll be living here with us. Period!"

This is where I should live? Hiiiieeeeeeer? My mom wasn't nice, the place stank, and I wasn't too comfortable with Jens, even though he was nice to me. After her announcement, nothing could hold me back. I screamed and cried, fell to my knees and drummed on the floor with my little fists: "I want to go to my grandma and my grandpa ... please ... please ... please ... d ... it's ... nice there and ... also in ..." I couldn't say any more. Mom pulled me up by the arm and slapped my bottom: "That's enough of the shouting, Cecilia. You're barely here and you're already making such a fuss," she shouted at me. Jens shouted: "Be quiet with the little one, she has to get used to the idea first." Shaking his head, he walked past mom, came to me and took me in his arms: "Hey Cecilia, calm down. All beginnings are hard, I understand that. You'll be going back to Grandma and Grandpa later ..." He didn't get any further, I interrupted him immediately.

"Yes ... u ... and there ... I want to stay!" I demanded, sobbing.

"But that's not possible. You're mom's child and your grandparents are getting older. But you know what? We'll go and visit them as often as we can, okay?"

What was left for me? I nodded politely and calmed down a little. That evening we had chips with ketchup and nuggets. Jens prepared the food. At the time, I didn't know that my mother couldn't cook at all. After dinner, we finally went back to my grandparents' house. But my perfect childhood world had been torn apart. I could hardly laugh anymore and didn't feel like doing anything. My childminder at the kindergarten spoke to my grandma about this and explained the new circumstances that affected me. She looked at me sympathetically and tried to encourage me by telling me how great it would be with my mother and her boyfriend.

I could clearly see that everyone around me was sad. My grandma cried a lot at that time, my grandpa was often alone in the garden, my friends didn't understand why I didn't want to play anymore and just sat alone in a corner. Nevertheless, I had the feeling that nobody understood me anyway. The adults ruled over me and I had to submit and be good. It was as simple as that.

I thought about simply running away. But where would I go? I would definitely be brought back immediately. I was still too small to do anything to myself, I couldn't think about that yet. What was I supposed to do?

Every day I begged grandma and grandpa not to give me away, to keep me with them, but they didn't stand a chance either. They weren't too old yet and could easily have raised me. It was just an excuse. My mother had custody and there was only a verbal agreement between them that I would live with grandma and grandpa for the time being. So it was easy to bring me "home" again.

It went back and forth for a few weeks. Mom would pick me up and bring me back in the evening. More and more often, however, I had to spend the night at her place. It was a horror. At my grandparents' I had a nice big room with fresh, nice-looking children's bed linen, everything was super clean and the room was flooded with light through the large window.

Here at mom's, I had a very small room with an old

wardrobe and a mattress. A mini window, which didn't really deserve the name, and I didn't have nice bed linen either. I loved snuggling up in my comforter when I was read stories. Not here. No one read me stories here at mummy's anymore and I didn't want to snuggle up in this blanket either. It wasn't as soft and fluffy as at Grandma's. It also smelled unpleasant.

Every time Mom came to get me, I cried like crazy. I fought tooth and nail. My grandparents tried to persuade my mother to leave me with them after all. But she wouldn't let them talk to her. I had to go with her.

At some point, the visits ended and I had to say goodbye to grandma and grandpa for good. It was the worst day of my life up to that point. We said goodbye to each other in tears. My grandpa, a grown, tall and proud man, cried like a child. What will it be like for them without me? Did they miss me? Were they happy that I was gone? No, I immediately pushed that thought away. They loved me, I knew that for sure.

My grandpa had packed me a big bag with all my toys. The first blow came straight away - I wasn't allowed to take it with me. "It won't fit in here. Our apartment is too small." I wasn't allowed to take all my fancy clothes with me either: "She'll grow out of everything quickly, where am I supposed to put all this stuff? We don't have much space." I looked at Grandma in despair, she shook her head in resignation and tried one last time: "Beate, leave Cecilia here. You can come and visit her at any time. Please, don't take her away from us, she's happy here. We'll do anything for her."

"No, mom, we've talked about this a thousand times. I want

my daughter with me ... we'll come and visit you."
All my belongings were stowed away in a small travel bag. Underwear, a dress, a pair of trousers, T-shirts and sweaters, my favorite doll and some dough. That was all I was allowed to take with me. I was just five years old and no longer understood the world. My day consisted of tears, tears, tears. My mother had no patience with me, she immediately snapped at me to stop crying.
Jens cleared out my bag with me and put everything away in the old, filthy cupboard in my room. He put the few toys on the floor and pulled out a coloring book, pencils and a drawing pad. "This is for you for moving in, sweetie." I tried to smile miserably, but it only turned into a wry grin. I was just desperate and unhappy. I got the only dress I was allowed to take with me from the wardrobe and took it to my "bed". I held it close to my face and smelled it. The smells took me back to grandma and grandpa. It smelled of fresh laundry and also somehow of my grandma. The bitterest tears flowed into the dress, that night I cried it wet.
I wasn't woken up lovingly the next morning. Grandma always came to my bed and stroked me with the words: "Mummy, get up, the sun is shining and it's sure to be a nice day" or: "It's raining today, but it's sure to be a nice day anyway." Then she would pull up the shutters: "Come on, I've got breakfast ready." Sometimes there were pancakes, but the rule was fresh rolls, jam and hot chocolate.
Everything was different with mom. She came in, commanded: "Get up, come on!" and was gone again. For breakfast we had an untoasted slice of white bread with jam, no cocoa, no tea, nothing. "I'm thirsty," my mother put a glass of water from the tap in front of me. Jens was sitting

at the table in a bad mood, as was my mother. Both were very quiet and stared ahead of them. Oh my God, I was going to have to stay here forever? My tears came again. "Don't whine again. What's wrong again?" she whined at me. I couldn't get a word out, for the first time in my life I was really scared. Not a normal fear of the dark, which I sometimes had with grandma and grandpa, or a fear of bugs, no. I was afraid of mum and Jens. I was afraid of Mom and Jens, they were weird. It wasn't possible for me to judge them at my age, but the fear was there.

I had been living with my mother for a week and was becoming increasingly quiet and anxious. Today I went to the new kindergarten for the first time. I wasn't dressed nicely. I hadn't had any nice, clean clothes since I'd been living with my mother. What I got from Grandma was now dirty and no longer smelled good. Mom didn't care. She put me in some clothes and off we went. I didn't feel well at all, but it didn't matter. I didn't have a chance to change anything.
"Take good care of the road, tomorrow you're going alone. It's not far." Startled, I looked at her: "Mom, I can't do that yet. I'm afraid to go alone."
"Nonsense, don't be like that. It's really not far and it's really easy to find." In the end, it was, but I envied the other children who were brought by their moms or dads and waved goodbye with a kiss and a wave. I hardly spoke at all. I withdrew completely. Every morning I crawled out of bed and gathered a few clothes, trembling with fear because I knew my mother would scold me again for the way I was dressed. There were times when I wore two different pairs of socks and put my shirt or pants on inside out. She always

got upset about it instead of taking my clothes out. I was still little and didn't know any better. I hardly ever had breakfast, if I did, it was a bit of muesli. Kindergarten was terrible for me. I loved going to the other nursery. Grandma always took me there, said goodbye lovingly and I played happily with the other children. Everything was different here. Nobody wanted to play with me. They teased me for being smelly and ugly. But I just wanted to fit in, I didn't stand a chance. My hair was long and curly, but now completely disheveled, my clothes were ugly and dirty. Nobody played with me at home or at kindergarten. What was suddenly so wrong with me? The nursery school teachers wanted to include me in the games, but they didn't stand a chance either. So I sat alone in a corner and played with a doll or Lego bricks. I was eager to paint and do handicrafts. I loved this activity.

I still don't have the words to describe how much I missed my grandparents. I missed the beautiful house, the wonderful garden, which always invited me to run around and play, so indescribably. There are no words to describe how I felt.

Homesickness
Longing
Despair
infinite grief

would not be sufficient.

We lived in a council apartment on the outskirts of the city. Many people here lived on the breadline. Nevertheless, I had the feeling that nobody was as unloving to their children as my parents were to me. Our furniture was completely old and unkempt - bulky garbage. Mom and Jens did nothing to make our home a bit more comfortable. Cleaning everything thoroughly and making the rooms look warm - unthinkable. They just sat around in a bad mood, but in the evening they became a bit more talkative and laughed.

There was garbage and dirty laundry everywhere. The ashtrays in the kitchen and living room were overflowing, dirty dishes were piled up in the kitchen. There were dried stains everywhere in the bathroom - in the bath, in the sink and on the floor. Our toilet was the only thing that was reasonably clean. Maybe it would have been normal for me if I didn't know any different. But I went from heaven to hell.

Mom also demanded that I address Jens as 'Dad'. It was strange at first, but I quickly got used to it. He was my dad and together they were now my parents. That was great! My mother exploded at me very quickly. Then she screamed at me and hit me. At first just on my bottom, the older I got, everywhere. I can no longer count the excuses: "Fell off my bike, fell down the stairs, ran into the door, etc.". The conditions at home became my little childhood normality. Sad, but unfortunately true.

Every night on my bed, I talked to Grandma and Grandpa. "Please, please ... bring me back to you. I'm always very well-behaved and always help with everything." I didn't want to have to stay here.

Neither of my parents worked. Nevertheless, it was unthinkable to have time for me. Our TV was on all day, my father smoked, drank and swore. My mother did the same.

I quickly realized that my parents drank a lot of alcohol. How often did I ask if I would get something to eat? "There's nothing out of line. Wait and see...!" Fresh fruit and vegetables were very, very rare.

My mother was either really cheerful, singing to herself or she was in a very bad mood. My father didn't hit me, but he was always in a bad mood too. Sometimes he laughed and joked with me though. It was rare, but at least he did it every now and then.

As I said, my clothes were in the wardrobe, but unsorted and almost never freshly washed. I only had worn-out clothes from second-hand stores. I don't want to badmouth these stores, but my clothes were unbeatable in terms of ugliness. No pretty colors, either too small or too big and shapeless. My grandma always said I was a very pretty girl with an angel's face and that I looked like a doll with my long hair. Her praise made me really proud. Now I just thought I was ugly and smelly. I wanted to crawl into a hole and never come out again. I was so ashamed of myself.

Several times a day I asked myself why Mom was so funny. Why did she sometimes sing to herself, why was she so full of good humor? When I crawled onto her lap at such times, she didn't push me away, no, she didn't do that. But she never put her arm around me or even cuddled me. I longed so much for security and love. But the mood always changed very quickly. I quickly lost hope that the good mood would last this time. From one moment to the next, she was in a bad mood, just grumbled to herself and shouted at me at every little thing.

Today I know why her moods changed so much, why she laughed and sang, why she swore and shouted and hit me, why she even slept again in the mornings. My mother was an alcoholic. She never admitted it, of course, but unfortunately that's the way it is.

I grew up with an alcoholic mother and a choleric stepfather who also drank. He wasn't as addicted to alcohol as my mother. My father didn't get drunk every day, but when he did, he really did. With my mother, it had to be wine in the morning, which later escalated into beer and schnapps; with him, it only started in the evening, but not every day.

All in all, from today's perspective, I had a cruel childhood from the age of five. I wanted love and security, but all I found was harshness, violence, dirt and alcohol. I wanted to love someone and I did. I loved my parents the way every child loves their parents - unconditionally and without demands. Unfortunately, I didn't get my love back. I blamed myself.
What was I doing wrong? Grandma and Grandpa loved me too. What was different about me now?
Why didn't my parents love me?
As a small child, I wanted to please my parents, I painted pictures, did handicrafts, proudly showed them or gave them presents, but recognition? Not a chance. It went in the bin: "What nonsense have you done again? Don't bother me with that crap ..." and so on and so forth. So I had to try even harder. Once, as a little girl, I tried to tidy up the kitchen and wash the dishes. To do this, I placed a chair by the sink, climbed up with my short little legs and tried to wash the dishes. I didn't know that you needed washing-up liquid for this. I simply held the plates and cups under the

tap. In this endeavor, I spread more wetness everywhere instead of cleaning the dishes. How was I supposed to be able to do it? The water ran down my arms and dripped onto the chair and down to the floor. My mother joined me, pulled me off the chair like crazy and slapped my bottom twice:
"What a mess, what are you stupid brat doing here? Everything is floating here."
"Mom ... i ... I ... wanted ... to ... help."
"Get out of your room and don't show your face again today!" Her eyes glared at me with infinite evil. I was hungry, but I didn't dare ask. Tears streamed down my little face and I trudged back to my room ashamed. I only wanted to be good and help. If mummy was sometimes so unwell that she had to sleep during the day, I should help, shouldn't I? Dad always said: "That's women's work." Dad cooked sometimes, he was good at it. Mom only had canned food, Dad cooked properly, it tasted good, but that was all he did. Tidying and cleaning was out of the question for him. He went shopping with us on Saturdays. A few groceries, cigarettes and alcohol. I had to walk silently alongside and for God's sake NEVER ask if I could have this or that. I tried a few times, of course, as all small children do. A fruit dwarf, a children's chocolate or an ice cream. Very banal little things. But I was hardly ever lucky. There was no money for that.
I literally had to learn the hard way that I had to keep my mouth shut when shopping, there were no wishes, BASTA!!!!

My fear of my parents grew and grew. Before every handshake I made, I panicked that it was wrong. I preferred to lie on my mattress and stare in front of me. A cheerful, curious child had turned into a scared, smelly little thing.

My parents were unhappy every day and almost all day long. This anxiety as a toddler got worse and worse over the years of my childhood and adolescence. My parental home became a horror for me. I can't describe it any other way.

I wanted love, security and protection. What did I get?

Fear, neglect, violence and worse.

Fear - fear is the only feeling I have and have had for as long as I can remember. Fear, panic and disgust haunt me to this day.

We never went to visit my grandparents and they never came to see us either. In the beginning, grandma and grandpa often called us and wanted to talk to me. At first I was allowed to, but because I kept begging them to please, please pick me up, my mother had had enough. She only very rarely allowed me to speak to my loved ones and when she did, I had to promise her in advance that I was fine and not to beg her to pick me up. It was so important to me to hear my grandma or grandpa that I promised everything she wanted to hear. I just begged in my mind for them to come and get me and every night on my mattress I talked to them. How I missed grandma and grandpa! Indescribable!

My parents' arguments escalated more and more. When I curled up in my bed for the night (I can't call it anything else), closed my eyes and shivered, I could hear them shouting. One evening, shortly before I started school, I saw my father beating my mother for the first time.
We had just finished dinner when my father threw his spoon across the kitchen. I stared at him in shock. My mother continued to eat calmly.
"For fuck's sake, Beate, can't you cook something decent ONCE? Every day such ready-made food!" he shouted at her, his eyes wide open. He continued to shout: "Why am I still here? Look at you, you bitch. And anyway, what a shithole this place looks like! You're a dirty cow!"
I sat frozen in my chair, usually shaking. I wanted to leave,

to get out of the kitchen, but I sat in my seat as if bolted down. Suddenly my dad jumped up angrily and the chair behind him tipped over. My mother was also startled and stopped eating abruptly. She also jumped up. Dad grabbed my mother's neck with one hand and kept hitting her in the face with the other. I cried louder and louder and shouted: "Stop it! B ... Bi ... Please ... stop ...!" I sobbed and screamed helplessly.

"You're a wreck," he shouted at her, and after a few blows to her face, he finally let go of her and disappeared from the kitchen. She was bleeding from the nose, her face was bright red, one eye was already swelling up and she was crying. I also had tears streaming down my face and snot running out of my nose. But instead of calming me down or even comforting me, my mother snapped at me: "Go to your room!"

Sobbing, I replied: "Dad is evil."

No sooner had I said it than her hand smashed into my face. I almost fell backwards in shock.

"That's no way to talk about your father. Off to your bed!"

I no longer understood the world. Dad had just been angry, what did I say that was wrong? I wanted to stand by her. I ran into my room crying, threw myself onto my mattress and pondered what I had done wrong again. A short time later, I heard my parents talking normally, even laughing together. How nice, I wanted to be there and laugh with them. I cautiously entered the living room; there were empty bottles and glasses on the table. That wasn't unusual for us, so I didn't think anything of it. Unfortunately, as always, I was annoying. "Off to bed!" was the only thing I heard.

Why didn't anyone comfort me? Why didn't they include me in their fun? Was I not one of them? What evil had I done?

I stood in the room, undecided, until Dad shouted at me: "Don't you hear me? Off you go!" I did as I was told. I didn't cry again that evening. I never wanted to cry again. I wanted to be strong, yes, and I didn't want to annoy my parents any more. That had to work. After all, I was no longer a baby. I NEVER succeeded. This goal was pointless. I could never please them. My mere presence was enough to infuriate them. Why? I was their child! What was so wrong with me? So I decided to try even harder not to stand out and to keep my mouth shut.

My first day at school was getting closer and closer. On the one hand, I was looking forward to going to school, but on the other hand, it scared me. What were the other children like to me? I made a firm resolution to always wash myself thoroughly. But what could I do about my unkempt and smelly clothes? I thought about it more and more often. There was only one way: I had to talk to my mother about it. I plucked up all my courage when she seemed in a good mood: "Mom?"

"What?" she asked impatiently.

"Can I get nice, clean clothes for school? Otherwise the other children will tease me again."

"Tell me, are you crazy?" At her words, she pulled me painfully by the arm all the way into my room. There she ripped open the wardrobe and threw all my things on the floor.

"Look at that pile of clothes! Isn't that enough for little Madame?" I started to tremble again, but I didn't want to give up just yet.

"But they're all old, creased, smelly and ugly."

Now it was over. She punched me in the face with full force.

"Then fold everything up nicely and it'll be neat and tidy. Maybe you brat will make demands too. What's there is enough! You'll get a dress for school and the rest will be good enough."

"It ... sti ... stinks ... but ... Ma ... Mama," I tried again, sobbing and stuttering.

My mother went crazy. She took the pile of laundry in her arms and raced into the bathroom. There she angrily threw all my clothes into the dirty bathtub, poured detergent over them and ran the water in.

"There you go, madame, then wash everything!"

I stood there, helpless and trembling. I was seven years old and didn't have the slightest idea how to do laundry. Besides, we had a washing machine.

"W ... wa ... why don't ... you do it ... i ... in ... the washing machine?" I sobbed desperately.

"Because it's not necessary. So get to work, Princess!"

I was standing there alone in the bathroom, the bathtub full of wet laundry. What was I supposed to do now? Sobbing, I bent down, took the first item and rubbed it between my hands, wrung it out and threw it on the floor. Where was I supposed to put the 'washed' laundry? I had no idea. Piece by piece, that's what I did. I can't remember how long I was busy. Suddenly my father stood in the room. "What are you doing here?" he shouted at me. My whole body immediately shook with fear. Trembling and with a shaky, thin voice, I replied: "... I have to ... do my ... laundry ... mom ...

said." I could bury this wish to stop crying. I couldn't do anything else. Always commands, beatings and scolding. How else was I supposed to deal with it as a little girl? I was doing everything wrong, even though I wanted to try so hard. All I wanted was to smell good and not have such stupid clothes for school.
"What, here in the bathtub and you alone?"
I nodded anxiously. My father stomped out of the bathroom angrily, shouting at my mother: "Are you going completely crazy now? A bathtub full of laundry and the child has to wash it by hand? Stop it now! You wash the laundry in the washing machine immediately and leave the little one alone!"
"Yes, but if she's constantly rebelling, stinking up the laundry and blah blah blah, she has to feel it too," Mom trumped up. I sat in front of the bath with my knees pressed tightly against my body and waited, crying, for what was to come. My father spoke calmly but threateningly: "If you don't get your ass to the washing machine right now and start washing your clothes, something will happen here. IMMEDIATELY!" I could tell from his voice that it was quiet, but seething with anger.
"Yes, that's all right," Mum barked and came into the bathroom.
"Did you do it again? Dad is angry with me and why? Because the miss is not satisfied with anything. Well done ... now get out of my sight!"
"Mom?" I whispered.
"Get lost!" was all I heard.
I bravely continued: "Can you show me how to use the washing machine? Then I can do it myself and help you."

"That's all that was missing. That you ruin everything for me. Get out of here, you redhead!" Ashamed, I trotted off to my room. Her constantly insulting words hurt my little soul so much. As usual, I lay trembling on my mattress. But one thing made me happy, Dad had stood by me and not made me do all the washing. Thank goodness. Mom had also said I would get a dress for school. I hope that comes true. As bad as my home was for me, I always hoped that everything would get better. Dad stood up for me today, so maybe that was a good sign. As we all know, hope dies last. Of course, I was also looking forward to a new dress. I wanted to be really smart for my first day at school.

We rarely had visitors. Grandma and Grandpa came sometimes, but they didn't feel comfortable with us. The fact that I could always visit them, as I had been promised, was also on hold. I'd only been to see my grandma and grandpa once since I'd been living with my mom. But everything was different. I didn't feel like playing in the sandpit or swinging. I ate my grandma's cake with a big appetite, I was almost always hungry. But otherwise I had become a different child. They didn't say anything to me, but they did to my mother. I noticed that.
"What's wrong with Cecilia? I've never seen her so quiet and listless. Is she all right?"
"Yes, she's fine. She's a bit scared of school," my mother said.
"She's also become so thin," Grandpa noted.
"Yes, because all she does is nag. Nothing is good enough for the good lady. You've spoiled her rotten," mom grumbled. I sat there impassively and just listened. I wasn't a

fussy eater, but unfortunately I rarely had a decent meal. I didn't dare say anything about it. My grandma asked me if I was already looking forward to starting school. I shook my head cautiously and ran into the garden. Tears were already making their way down my face again, I didn't want anyone to see them. The question of whether my grandma could take me shopping for a nice dress for my big day was immediately rejected.

"No, we'll take care of that, don't interfere everywhere!"
"But I only mean well, then you can save the money. We'll buy her some fancy shoes too."
"Hell no. We'll do it!" Mom was very annoyed again.
How I would have loved to go shopping with grandma and grandpa. I always had nice clothes to wear with them. But well, Mom had promised to get me a new dress from her, then I would certainly be all dressed up. That evening, I begged to be allowed to stay with my grandparents for the night. Nothing, no chance. To this day, I still don't know why my mother never let me. Grandma and Grandpa. They would do anything for me, but their hands were tied here and this fact hurt deep in their hearts.

My big school enrollment day was getting closer and closer. Just two days to go. My parents took me shopping. Notebooks, pens and books. Then it was time for my outfit. Mom had promised me a new dress. I was really looking forward to it. I could already see myself in front of me - a beautiful pink or white dress, white socks and patent leather shoes. That's how I imagined my first day at school would look. But I was wrong. We went home.
"When are we going to buy my dress and shoes?" I asked,

completely excited because I was so looking forward to it. "We've already done that. Don't get on my nerves now!" my mother said caustically. They probably wanted to surprise me with it. Did they perhaps already have a sugar cone for me? Sure, they certainly did. Adults sometimes have secrets to surprise their children. My tummy was tingling with excitement and anticipation.

I slept very badly the night before. Not at all, actually. I was finally able to wear nice clothes.

It was finally here - today was my day. The sun's rays tickled my face. I got up, opened the tiny little window and greeted the beautiful morning: "Hello, dear sun, today is my big day. I'm going to school and I'm getting nice new clothes. Oh yes ... I'm so happy," I laughed into the sunny morning. I skipped happily to the kitchen. Today I had cornflakes with milk. The ones with honey were my favorite. I was beaming all over my face. But my parents were sitting at the table in a bad mood. They didn't greet me warmly, no, they weren't happy with me. This fact was the first damper on my joy. It was as if my new path in life was none of their business. They didn't ask me anything, didn't say a word to me. But I didn't want to let them spoil my good mood just yet. I didn't want my excitement about school to be dampened.

"Wash and brush your teeth," my mother ordered me. Now I was about to get my new dress. Hundreds of butterflies danced with joy in my little belly. My mother laid out my clothes for me to wear on my special day. When I saw the dress, I was stunned, seconds later tears came to my eyes. It was so ugly and absolutely not new, as she had promised.

Black with gray stripes. I wore ugly brown sandals and my hair was lovelessly tied up in a ponytail. No bow in my hair, no frills on the dress, nothing. No white tights or white socks. I would have preferred not to go to my first day of school at all, I was already so ashamed. My father wordlessly handed me a small sugar cone. I was a bit happy about that, although I thought I would get one of the nice, big, fancy ones I had seen in the stores. But we didn't have much money, I had to understand that. I wish I at least had a nice dress, I didn't care about anything else.

My grandparents came to my special day. My grandma looked at me in shock, then looked at my mother: "Is that how you want my angel to go to her special day?"

"Yes, she can wear the dress again and again and it suits her," replied Mum listlessly.

My grandma hugged me tightly, her eyes were moist. When my grandpa came in, he had a big sugar cone in his hand, which he handed to me. There was a cuddly toy at the top. I was delighted. It was the big one I had always wanted. Pink with a little horse on it. But which one should I take to school? Dad took the answer away from me.

"You take the big school bag with you, the other one is for home." They also gave me a new school bag. It was so beautiful, also pink with little white horses on it. But my outfit was so awful that I didn't really want to go to school. But I had a big school bag, I wondered curiously what was in it. My grandparents said almost nothing, I think they were completely stunned by my appearance. Finally, we set off. We had barely arrived when I wanted to sink to the ground in shame. No girl was dressed like me. They all had fancy dresses on, bows in their hair and beautiful sandals or patent leather shoes. I was incredibly embarrassed about my appearance. If I hadn't been so scared of my parents, I would have let my tears run free. I just wanted to go home. I can still feel the mean and disparaging looks from the other children today. It was now clear to me that I no longer had the slightest desire to go to school. Everything rushed past me that day. All the parents were taking photos of their children, taking photos with their parents and grandparents. That didn't happen with me. My father took just one photo, which I still have. It doesn't show a happy child in nice clothes, beaming with joy at school. I look into the camera, serious and unkempt with my school bag. My face speaks volumes. Why didn't my grandparents take a photo? They didn't want to record this misery forever. They felt sorry for me, I know that today.

I had coffee and cake at home and my parents showed no interest in this important day for their child. I would never make friends. I was aware of that. I went back to my bed and cried in despair. I was helpless, unfortunately there was nothing I could do about my appearance. My first day at school was an infinitely sad day for me, unfortunately my grandparents couldn't do anything about it. They had tried, but my mother blocked everything.

No other child in my class was dressed like me. Although everyone else who lived near us was also poor, nobody wore such ugly clothes. While I wore worn-out clothes from the second-hand store, patched pants and jackets, the other children were dressed almost smartly in contrast to me. The girls' hair had fancy hair clips or ribbons. Today, of course, I know that such things didn't cost much money. My parents just weren't interested or were they deliberately trying to humiliate me? They succeeded perfectly. Nobody wanted to sit next to me at school. During the breaks, all the children had delicious school sandwiches, small carrots or cucumber and a chocolate bar or another tasty sweet. If I was lucky, I sometimes had an apple or a banana. But not every day. Even today, I still feel lost and desperate.

In the first week, my mother took me to school and picked me up again. Then I had to walk on my own.

Although I hated school, I wanted to learn well. Maybe the other children would play with me if I did well. They would realize that I wasn't stupid. This plan failed miserably. I didn't have my own table or even a desk at home. I had to do my homework at the kitchen table. My mother sat next to it with her wine and stared holes in the air. She showed no interest whatsoever in my homework or what I had learned at school. But if she did look over my homework or even Dad, then the circus was on. If I didn't understand something or didn't have an answer to a question, if I hadn't written properly, my mother would take a spoon out of the drawer, hold it by the handle and flick the other side against my head. She called this action "spooning". The pain was unbearable. I'm lucky that I never had a hole in my head, but this terrible measure left me with painful bumps. I was so scared that I often couldn't give the right answers or kept prescribing myself. I was already shaking beforehand. I never received any praise or encouragement. I thoroughly lost the joy of learning.

Every single day on the way home, I wondered if mom had prepared something to eat or if she was in a bad mood. I didn't have my own key, so I had to ring the doorbell. When my father opened the door, I knew that mom was either asleep or sitting listlessly on the sofa with empty beer bottles in front of her. When Dad was in a good mood, he would make me cornflakes or eggs, but that rarely happened. I was still small, but completely on my own. The only thing my parents gave me throughout my childhood and adolescence was a roof over my head and a place to sleep. Regular, healthy meals, a daily shower and fresh laundry were not on the agenda.

I felt more and more that my parents didn't love me. But I longed for it so much, I wanted to love and be loved. Even at school, I noticed the stark difference between me and the other children. At the end of the school day, they all ran to the gate like frightened chickens, were picked up by a parent, kissed and hugged. Why didn't mom or dad do that? Not once.

How I longed for grandma and grandpa. Everything would have been so nice there, I would have clean and nice smelling things and I would always get praise when I did something well. If I didn't understand something, my grandpa would explain everything to me calmly and precisely. Almost every day I cried bitterly with longing for the two dearest people I hardly ever got to see again. I made up my mind that when I grew up, I would go and see them, just like that. No matter whether my parents liked it or not. When I grew up, they wouldn't be able to tell me anything. I would just go and live with grandma and grandpa and be done with it. That became my goal.

I got through school year after school year more badly than well. I was definitely an outsider. I wasn't included in any activities. It was painful to hear the other children chattering about their birthday parties. There were presents, cake, chips, spaghetti with tomato sauce. Games were played and there were even small prizes to be won. I was never there. I would like to emphasize once again that none of the people around me were rich, but no parents were as indifferent and indifferent to their children as mine. Many children also wore second-hand clothes, but they weren't dressed ugly, unlike me. Trying to shine by doing well also went down the drain. The only subject I was good at was design. I still loved to paint. My pictures were always praised. I had a few coloring books at home, but coloring was no longer enough for me. Dad got me drawing pads and pencils so that I could draw whatever I wanted. I painted my grandparents' garden in all its variations, I painted every room in the house, my room, which I had at Grandma's house. It made me feel close to them both. It hurt so terribly to only be allowed to paint the home of my dear grandma and grandpa, to no longer live there, it was hell. I missed them so indescribably.

I was now ten years old and in the fourth grade. The situation at home didn't change, if anything it got worse and worse.
My mother was often unwell in the last few weeks. She slept even more than usual, her body was shaken by nausea and vomiting. Could she no longer tolerate the alcohol? Maybe she would stop drinking and then be kind to me?
We sat down to dinner and had noodle soup. I always had to add Maggi to my plate for soup, it tasted better. Lots of Maggi, the soup turned brown, I loved it that way. Suddenly, my father hit the table so loudly with the flat of his

hand that the Maggi bottle fell out of my hand in shock and landed in the soup in front of me. "Do you always have to take so much of that stuff? It all costs money, Cecilia," he raged. Startled, I looked at my mother, but she didn't make a move. She just looked at her husband and remained silent. My father continued to rage: "Look at the mess now, the Maggi bottle in the soup. I'm going to go crazy, clean it up now!"

I took the bottle out of the soup with two fingers, it was dripping of course, but I didn't think that far ahead. I got up and wanted to take the bottle to the sink to rinse it off. As I stood up, I knocked my plate and its contents to the floor. "Ent ... sorry ... sorry ... I ... I ... m ... do that ... gl ... right away," I stammered, terrified and already trembling with fear. My mother jumped up, grabbed me by the arm and immediately hit me: "You're a real dirty pig. Look at that mess, you're really too stupid to eat normally." Her hands kept hitting the back of my head, my back and my bottom. She hit everywhere but my face. She didn't dare, because a teacher at school might notice. I screamed and cried, hoping my father could intervene and protect me. Nothing happened, he sat calmly at the table and watched the goings-on impassively. He didn't help me in my distress and agony. Did he enjoy her beating me up and he could watch the spectacle? I was a child, didn't he have to protect me? When my mother had had her fill, she kicked me hard in the butt and shouted: "Off to your room, don't show your face again today!"

Crying and writhing in pain, I crept into my "realm". My attempt to carefully lie down on my bed failed. My body hurt so incredibly. With difficulty, I turned onto my stomach, a position that was somewhat bearable.

When I had calmed down, I heard my parents arguing loudly.

"I can't do this," my mother cried.

"Nonsense, what do you have to do all day? Cecilia and the little bit of housework are too much for you? You drink all day and let everything go to rack and ruin!" Dad scolded loudly.

"Then why don't you do it when you're better at it," replied mom. Then there was a clap. Trembling with fear, I was still lying on my stomach and listening. Mom was crying loudly now, suddenly there was a clang. Over and over again. What was going on? I was scared, but at the same time I wanted to know what was happening at my parents' house. I got up carefully and crept to the kitchen, where the noises were coming from. Mom was sitting at the kitchen table and crying, holding a handkerchief to her nose. She was bleeding. My father was angrily throwing dishes against the wall. Terrified, I turned around and scampered back to my room. Great fear spread through me again. After what felt like an eternity, it was quiet. I bravely left my room, went into the living room and wanted to sit next to my mother. Even before I sat down, Mom blurted out: "I'm pregnant." Is that why she had been feeling so bad recently? Is that why she was throwing up so often? Is it okay to drink alcohol then? I was only ten years old, but when a little baby is growing in your belly, you have to eat healthily, don't you? The little one needs everything that is important for healthy development. I was fully aware of this and I also knew that alcohol was not beneficial. At that moment, I couldn't deal with my mother's statement. I paused in my movement and waited to see what would happen. I looked at my father, who was sitting wide-eyed in his armchair. Mom looked at him anxiously. He jumped up in one leap and with long strides was at my mother, bent down to her and pulled her into his arms. "You're pregnant? Honey, that's wonderful," he rejoiced. But mom fought him off, squirming out of his embrace.

"I don't want another child. I've had enough of this brat," she said, pointing her index finger at me derogatorily. I flinched almost imperceptibly. Her words hurt so much. But Dad wasn't deterred. He waved me over, took me on his lap and put his arm around my mother.

"We can manage that. Cecilia is almost a big girl and can help you. Hey ... we're a family after all." A short pause, then he continued: "So from today, everything will be different. Healthy food, no more alcohol for you, darling, and we'll clean up properly every day." At that moment, with Dad on my lap and his kind words, I felt safe and secure. Suddenly my mother jumped up and I fell to the floor in shock.

She screamed: "I! WILL! NO! BALG! MORE! No more alcohol for me? Clean every day? Aha? And the fine gentleman carries on as usual? Nope, without me. I'm going to have an abortion. That's it!"

"No, you won't. We're having this baby and yes, no more alcohol for you."

"Forget it!" mom yelled.

Dad jumped up, rumbled towards her and slapped her twice. One right and one left, her head flew back and forth from the force of the blow and her nose bled again. Dad continued to shout: "What I say still happens here. A baby is a miracle and we're going to have it too!"

"What kind of man hits a pregnant woman?" I asked myself, startled. "Dad, Mom's having a baby, stop hitting her!" I blurted out bravely.

"And where should it sleep? We have no room and no money," my mother protested, but now weakly, she was afraid of her husband.

"First in our bedroom while it's still so small and then we'll see." Mom didn't say anything more. I wanted to go to her, to comfort her. "Mom...", I whispered.

"Stay away from me now," I heard her soft voice. Disappointed and rejected again, I sprinted to my room. Still in pain, I lay down on my mattress and tried to process what I had just seen and heard. Mom had a baby, Dad beat her, broke dishes and I was just in the way and costing money anyway. They didn't even look after me properly. I lay there for an eternity, fell asleep briefly and woke up hungry. Dinner was already over and I had eaten next to nothing due to my mishap. Hungry, I crept into the kitchen at night. I wanted to make myself a cheese sandwich. I was trying so hard not to make any noise, concentrating so hard on it that I didn't even notice Dad at first. Suddenly he was standing behind me: "What are you doing here at this time of night?" "I'm hungry," I replied quietly. I was prepared for anger and shouting, but nothing of the sort happened.

"Sit down at the table, I'll make you something. Would you like scrambled eggs?" Oh yes, as hungry as I was, I was delighted. I nodded, beaming. Dad smiled at me and winked his eye: "Well, I'll do that then." It smelled and tasted heavenly. We both sat at the table and ate in silence. I became brave.

"Dad?"

"Yes, mouse?"

What was wrong with him? He was in such a good mood and there for me? Anyway, I wanted to take advantage of the situation and get some answers.

"Is mom having the baby?"

"Yes, of course, then you're the big sister," he smiled.

"But ... but mom doesn't want it at all."

"Yes, yes, it'll be fine, we just have to help her a little, then it'll work out."

"But she always scolds me and when I want to help, I always do everything wrong." Tears stung my eyes again.

"Then you'll just have to try harder, Princess. We'll manage. Are you looking forward to having a sibling?"

"Oh yes, I can love and cuddle it," I said happily.

Dad laughed: "Yes, but a baby isn't a doll, there's more to it than that. Feeding, changing, going out into the fresh air and so on and so forth."

"I want to do everything," I trumpeted.

"Well, that's nice. Only school mustn't suffer. I mean ... not just seeing the baby and so on, but also thinking about school." I nodded, but didn't really understand his words. I shouldn't neglect school? My parents hadn't cared about my performance until now. No one even paid attention to the order of my exercise books and books. I didn't know how to do it on my own, but I made a great effort. I didn't even have any envelopes. My parents didn't show me how to do it. Was that really going to change? A new baby and my life would get better? That's how much I wanted to believe and I did.

The pregnancy was completely normal. But what surprised me was that my mother never went to the doctor. Don't you have to have a check-up to make sure everything is OK with the baby? There are examinations where you can see the little one on the screen. That's strange. Worse still, she continued to drink alcohol and smoke cigarettes. My father did the same. That worried me a lot.

As always, I came home from school with a bad feeling. Will mom be awake? Is she in a bad mood? Today was the last day of school before the summer vacation. A reason for joy for so many children. How much I envied them all. The children were allowed to visit their grandparents or had fun with their siblings. I sat at home, had to be insulted and beaten and, on top of that, watch my parents drink alcohol, let the apartment fall into disrepair and did nothing, nothing at all, with me. My report card was anything but good, I had poor grades. So scolding or maybe even beatings were inevitable. The closer I got to home, the faster my heart beat. I rang the bell as I still wasn't allowed to have a key. Dad opened the door for me. Okay, Mom was probably asleep. I put down my satchel and saw Mom staggering out of the kitchen. She smiled at me and slurred, "Oh, you're here already? Is it that late already?" My heart raced so that I could feel it beating in my throat. Fear crept up inside me. My mother was completely drunk again at lunchtime. Now she was also asking for my report card. I would like to emphasize once again that I NEVER had help with my schoolwork. It didn't matter whether I had mastered the subject matter or not. I did everything on my own, and that's what my report card looked like. Poor performance in almost all subjects.

I dug my school report out of my satchel and held it out to her. She took it and looked at it. Her smile died immediately. I stood anxiously in front of my parents. Mom looked at Dad, angrily handed him the proof of my unspeakable achievements and Dad got angry too:

"What's that, Cecilia? Tell me, are you still okay? Are you crazy? Why don't you learn more if you can't understand it?"

I looked down at the floor, ashamed and afraid. I didn't know what to say and didn't dare. I wanted to scream, '... then help me!' Before I knew it, my mother's hand slammed right into my face. My head flew to the side and I held my burning cheek, terrified. No, please don't cry now. I didn't want them to see my tears.

"Make sure you get to your room and don't show your face again today!" my mother yelled at me, slurring her words. Before I went to my room, she kicked me so hard in the butt that I thought my tailbone was cracked. I threw myself onto my bed on my stomach and finally let my tears flow freely. Yes, my report card was bad, but shouldn't my parents try to do something about it with me? Learn with me, explain things to me, simply help me?

I had just calmed down when my dad stood in my room. He took my satchel, opened it and looked inside: "What's this mess?" he shouted. At his words, he turned my school bag over and tipped the contents onto the floor. Crumpled and loose sheets of paper, books with stains and dog-ears and pens landed on the dirty floor in front of me. I looked at him in shock. Dad stood calmly in front of my "camp". He slowly picked up a book and hit me hard on the back of the head. "Ouch ... Dad ...", I gasped, I was so startled. My hand held the sore spot.

"What kind of order do you have in your school things? Miss, surely that's the least you can ask? Tidiness! But things will be different next school year, princess, otherwise it's going to get really messy." I was getting brave now.

"Dad, I need envelopes for the books and exercise books, a new pencil case, a new ink box and more loose-leaf binders." I looked at him anxiously now, but he suddenly sat down quietly with me. He stroked my head and pulled me close. It was very unusual, but I enjoyed the moment to the very fiber of my heart. I longed so much for security and love. "I promise we'll get you everything you need for the new school year, okay?"

I smiled gratefully at him and nodded. "Can you also help me with tasks that I don't understand?" Dad nodded with a smile: "Of course. The baby will be here soon, so we have to support mom, and if you help mom diligently, then I'll help you, is that a deal?"

"Yes," I whispered gratefully. I was so happy at that moment, but Dad stopped stroking my head and his hand moved lower and lower. He stroked my thighs. Nothing wrong with that, so I still enjoyed his stroking. "I love you so much, my little princess," he breathed into my ear.

"I love you too, Dad."

I was only wearing a light dress because it was so warm, so it was easy for his hand to reach my knickers. I was rigid with fear. What was he doing? Is he allowed to do that? "You're very special. Daddy loves you very much." His voice became a little frantic. Suddenly, I felt my panties being pushed to the side and Dad pushing me backwards onto my bed. He stroked me between my legs, it was so uncomfortable, I felt ashamed. "Daddy ... what ... are ... you doing?"

"I'll show you how much I love you. That's what dads do." Should that really be normal? All dads do it like this? His stroking became faster and faster, his breathing became louder and louder. I lay there very still, afraid I couldn't move. Now he groaned loudly a few times, then he took his hand off me.

"Not a word to your mother! Don't you dare say a word about it and a disaster will happen here. I just want to show you how much I love you and you'll show me how much you love me more in the future too, yeah? That will be our sweet secret."

His tone was very demanding and strict on the one hand, but also somehow kind on the other. I was torn between the two. I looked at him helplessly and nodded. He leaned over me, stroked my cheek: "That's sweet, my little princess", got up and left. I was still lying motionless on my mattress. What was that all about? Stroking is wonderful, but between my legs? That was disgusting and incredibly embarrassing. Was I normal? No, I certainly wasn't normal, Dad will be right if he demands my love too. That was the way it was, wasn't it? Parents loved their children and children loved their parents. Then you have to show that to each other.

Deep inside me, however, resentment, horror and fear spread. Somehow I suspected that this was NOT normal. But no matter, I would do anything for a little love and security and if he wanted to stroke me all over, then he should. There were worse things.

I had been keeping a diary for a long time. No, I didn't have one, I used my German exercise books for it. I had enough of them so that it wasn't noticeable. I hid it between my other notebooks.

I don't want to write all my diary entries here, just this one that I wrote after my father's horrific actions:

Date

Dear diary,

Today I got into a lot of trouble because of my bad report card. Mom hit me again and kicked me once. I was hungry at night and Dad was so kind and prepared scrambled eggs. It was so delicious. He was so sweet to me. He even stroked me everywhere. Even where I was so ashamed. Dear diary, do you know if this is normal? I want to do everything I can to make him love me and if THAT is part of it, then so be it.
Love
Love
Fear
Grandma and Grandpa, I miss you so much.
I have to become better and more diligent.

The disaster took its course.

I was different, very different from the other children, I felt that every day. Insecurity, disgust, fear and guilt are more or less the right words for me. The worst thing was my own cleanliness. My teacher once said to me that I should clean the dirt from under my fingernails and brush my hair more carefully. My clothes still weren't washed regularly either, of course I didn't dare say it at home anymore. Before gym class, it was hell. "Stinkie's changing", the children mocked me, holding their noses provocatively as they said it. When I wore my ugly sports clothes, which were far too small, they laughed at me: "Oooooh ... Madame went shopping ... was that available in your size and in chic?" It was so humiliating, but what was I supposed to do? I wanted nice clothes but couldn't get any. What I did decide to do was to wash my whole body every day and comb my hair nicely. However, I didn't take my parents into account. Every evening I went into the bathroom and turned on the bath. It felt so good to relax in the warm water, soap up and smell good. I did that for a week and it was so nice. I was lying relaxed in the bath again, daydreaming, when suddenly my mother stood in the bathroom: "What are you doing here?" I completely flinched in shock. "Washing and bathing myself." I immediately started shaking.
"Get out of the bath, you bitch! Do you know how much a full bath costs? You're out of your mind!"
"But mom ... I just ... want ... to smell good and ... be ... really ... clean."
"Have you ever heard of washcloths? You don't have to get

into the bath every day, Countess." I was still lying anxiously in the pleasantly warm water. Her hand landed on my face again. "Get out of the tub!" But I was paralyzed with fear and couldn't move. What bad thing had I done? Bathed myself? Was that so terrible? Mom grabbed my arm and tried to pull me out of the bath, but she slipped off my wet body. Then she just shouted: "I want you out of the bath, but very suddenly!" Her voice almost cracked, she was shouting so loudly.

"Yes ... Mom, I ... I'm already coming. Are you ... going out until then?"

"Well, you're going to waste even more water. You come out now and I'll stay here!" My ears were already buzzing from the volume. Why didn't Dad come and protect me? I wasn't doing anything wrong. I had no choice but to get out of the bath under their stern eyes and dry myself off. I wasn't dressed yet when the blows started raining down on me. She hit me everywhere, she didn't care where she hit me. The last blow to my head was so hard that I stumbled and hit my forehead on the sink. Luckily it wasn't quite that hard, otherwise who knows what could have happened. I kept crying and screaming for her to please stop. She threw my pyjamas at my feet and ordered me into my room. I pressed a towel to my head because it was bleeding a little. My lovely bath time today and the last few days were over. As always, I was only allowed to bathe once a week. From now on, only under my mother's supervision. I was allowed to use very little water. Just enough so that my legs were slightly under water, that was all. My mother washed my long hair with cold water. It was a horror. Nevertheless, I did everything I could to be clean and not stink. Every evening and every morning I washed myself with a washcloth and brushed my teeth properly. My hair was brushed and I felt a little better. But every time I put on my faded, old-fashioned clothes, which also smelled anything but good, this feeling disappeared. The children continued to tease me or ignore me. I could now claim that I had come to terms with the situation. But that would be a lie. You don't put up with being bullied for things you can't influence yourself. Nobody puts up with bullying at all. Only I would have liked to do everything I could to be clean and smell fresh, to get help with schoolwork, but unfortunately I had no chance in any way. Did I have any other choice?

One night I was woken up by a bad nightmare. At first I lay very still in bed, not daring to move. When I had composed myself a little, I switched on the light and thought about my misery. Suddenly the scales fell from my eyes. Why didn't I just go to grandma and grandpa? What were my parents going to do about it? But then what? Would I just be able to stay there? Would I have to go back? What would await me then? Beatings that I couldn't imagine in my worst dreams? And the baby? Once it was born, wouldn't I have to help mom?
Leave? Stay here? Leave? Stay here?
I decided to stay here. When I grew up, I still had my goal of going to my favorite people. Then no one could take me back. I would hold out here until then and soon I would have a little sibling that I could love and show and give my love to.

The birth of the baby was getting closer and closer. I

imagined life with a baby would be so beautiful. Everyone is happy, cheerful and proud.

My mother's belly was already taking on huge proportions, she complained every day that she could no longer bend over and that her fat belly was getting on her nerves. She wasn't looking forward to the little one at all. Not at all. There was a crib in my parents' bedroom, that was all there was for the little one. There were bottles in the kitchen cupboard and everything else in my parents' bedroom cupboard. There was no changing table, no place in the living room with a small blanket where the little one could lie. Nothing.

Antonia

I woke up in the night, mom was screaming in pain, dad was trying to calm her down. There was nothing keeping me in bed, it wasn't my parents fighting, so I wasn't afraid to leave my room. I ran to the voices coming from the bedroom. Mom was lying curled up on the bed and kept crying out at certain intervals, Dad was calling the ambulance, completely agitated. "What's wrong with mom?"
"The baby's coming," Dad told me. I ran to my mom and took her hand. "Does it hurt so much when mine has a baby?" I wanted to know. Mom nodded weakly and the pain started again. Mom screamed again. "I can't take it anymore, Jens." She was sweating profusely and writhing in pain. Finally the doorbell rang and help arrived. Mom was taken away and we were allowed to accompany her. At the hospital, however, I had to wait in the corridor, Dad stayed with my mother the whole time. It took hours. Nevertheless, I was looking forward to the baby. I kept looking at the clock, it seemed to me as if the hands weren't moving at all. After an eternity, my dad came to me: "You have a little sister."
"Yay, a sis ... oh dad, I'm so happy." The sparkle in my father's eyes delighted me. "When can I see it?" I asked impatiently.
"The baby will be checked and mom will be taken care of, then you can say hello to your little sister. I'll go and see her again and when the time comes, I'll come and get you, okay?"
"Is it taking that long again?" I asked impatiently.

"No, definitely not." He hurriedly went back to his wife and I sat alone again in this impersonal hospital corridor. Dad finally came to me. He was crying.

"Dad, what's wrong? What's wrong with mom?"

It took a while for him to calm down: "Cecilia, the baby is not completely healthy."

I looked at him in shock: "Oh dear Dad, does the baby have to stay here or have an operation?"

Dad shook his head sadly: "No, it will now be connected to devices that monitor it for twelve hours and if everything is OK, then nothing needs to be done." I was pleased: "Well, that's good. I don't understand what's wrong with the baby. Aren't all babies monitored thoroughly?"

Dad started crying again: "It's not a normal baby, Cecilia. Your sister has Down's syndrome. She won't be able to develop normally and will be mentally handicapped." RUMS! Excuse me? Mentally handicapped? I looked at my father with wide, startled eyes: "And you already know all that?"

He nodded and said quietly: "Yes, the doctors know that. But nobody can say how severe it will be in your sister's case. There are mild and severe cases, it only becomes clear when the baby develops how severe the ... syndrome ... is."

I didn't understand any of this and wanted to finally see the baby.

"You can't say hello to your sister today, but tomorrow, I promise. Do you still want to see mom?"

Yes, of course, I wanted that. Mom was lying in bed, her eyes were in deep sockets and completely teary. When she saw us, her gaze became fixed and she turned around so that we could only see her back. "Mom?" I whispered cautiously.

"Go away! I don't want to see anyone and be alone!"

Dad put his arm around me: "Beate ... darling ... we'll be back tomorrow." He didn't say any more and pulled me along with him.

We took the train home, each of us lost in our own thoughts. I had a disabled sister? Why? Why did mom never go to the doctor during her pregnancy? Could it have been prevented? Was the alcohol to blame, which Mom had continued to drink? So many questions - no answers.

"Dad, what was the name of that thing the baby has?"

"Down syndrome." That was all he said.

It was almost morning, we arrived home, nobody wanted to eat anything. I lay down, but sleeping was out of the question. I brooded and brooded. What was it going to be like now? Doesn't a disabled child need all the attention it can get? Do you have to take intensive care of it? Will other people laugh at it? I saw my little sister completely disfigured in front of me and suspected the worst. I actually didn't want to see the baby anymore. Can't you give it away then? If it's a little monster baby, we can't keep it, can we? No, I didn't want a deformed baby. And I didn't want one that would never be able to read or write and that I wouldn't be able to play with. NO!

I didn't want a deformed and mentally handicapped baby, BASTA!

Reluctantly, I went to the hospital with Dad the next day. There was a doctor at my mother's bedside when we entered. She greeted us kindly: "Yes, I've just explained it to your wife. Your daughter was monitored, a complete blood count was taken and her heart was examined. I can tell you that your daughter is completely healthy organically. Often babies with Down's syndrome have problems with their heart or intestines, but your daughter is fine," she beamed at us. Her words were something like that. I hardly listened because I didn't care what would happen to this child. I just didn't want it.

"Then it's the Sy ... um ... isn't it?" I asked hopefully.

The doctor squatted down, took my hands and smiled at me: "Down syndrome is the name of your little sister's condition. We can't say how severe the disability will be or how much her growth will be affected. But I promise you, you'll love the little one. She's sweet as sugar ... believe me." Well, she had a lot to say. I don't want a disabled sister, I will never be able to love her. NEVER! Nevertheless, I nodded in agreement.

Next to my mother's bed, a baby suddenly screamed, crying heartbreakingly. I looked around uncertainly. The doctor beamed at me: "Your little sister wants to say hello to you." 'BUT NOT ME', it screamed inside me.

My father went to the crib and carefully lifted the baby into his arms. Such a little bundle. My father became very quiet. I didn't want to see it, not to look at it, just not. Then I would always see the deformed baby, even if I closed my eyes, I would have this image of the disabled, horrible-looking baby in front of me.

"Would you like to hold her, Cecilia?" Dad asked.

"No," I said firmly.

"Come over here!" Dad sat down on my mother's bed. But I stood there as if nailed down and couldn't, wouldn't move.

"Don't be afraid, come here!" Unsure, I went to him after all, but looked into the void. I didn't want to look, I was afraid of what I would see.

"Cecilia, take it easy. I dare you." I shook my head.

'At least take a look at your sister,' Dad tried to persuade me. Mom didn't say a word, she just stared ahead of her. I struggled with myself, what should I do? I had to see her at some point, at the latest when she came home with Mum. I had no choice but to look at her at some point anyway. So I had to go through with it now. I looked carefully at the bundle in Dad's arm. Before I knew it, Dad was holding the baby in his arms. The little one's eyes were open and it seemed as if she was looking at me hard. I didn't see a deformed baby. Well, it looked a bit different, the eyes were a bit wide apart and looked a bit puffy, you could tell something was wrong, but she was still so cute. I fell in love with my little sister instantly. I carefully stroked her little fingers and ran my index finger over her little nose and cheeks. Her little lips and mini tongue moved as if she was sucking. All my rejection vanished into thin air. I looked happily at Dad: "She's so cute," I said, moved. I turned to mom: "Mom, I'll help you wherever I can. I want to be there for the baby whenever I can."

"Yes, then do it," she said emotionlessly.

"She'll have all my love, I promise." I wanted to put the baby in mummy's arms: "Go away with the brat!" she hurled at me quietly so that her bedmate couldn't hear. Startled, I held the baby even tighter in my arms. I found it incredibly difficult to part with her when we had to make our way home. I was so happy and so incredibly happy for my sister.

"Dad, what's her name supposed to be?"

He shrugged his shoulders: "Mom doesn't care and I don't

know. Do you have a suggestion?"

I thought about it for a moment and quickly came up with the sweetest name I could think of: "Antonia ... Toni for short," I beamed.

"Good, then the little one's name is Antonia," he agreed. We visited mom and Antonia in the hospital every day for a week. Mom hardly spoke a word and never held her baby in her arms when we were there. "Mom, doesn't Antonia need to feed at your breast?" I asked curiously. I wanted to see how sweetly she was breastfed by Mama.

A helpless little mouse like that needs to be fed.

"I don't have any milk and that's fine, I don't want to do this." Dad explained to me straight away: "Some mothers don't have any milk, Cecilia. But that's no problem, Antonia will get the bottle." I nodded.

"Antonia? What kind of name is that?" asked Mom indignantly.

"You didn't care, Cecilia and I just chose this name."

"What an ugly name," she scolded and then continued: "Well, ugly name, ugly baby." BANG! How could she talk like that? It was her baby. She had to love it and not talk so disparagingly.

"Pull yourself together now," Dad scolded quietly.

The day arrived, my little sister came home with mom. I was so happy.

"Dad, why don't we have a changing table and a baby bath?"

"Because we don't have the money for it. We can change her on the bed and she is still so small, we have a larger plastic bowl and later she can also be bathed in the bath, you just have to hold her firmly." I was satisfied with that explanation. I didn't know any better. My parents will do the right thing for the little mouse. Of course, my parents were given money for my little sibling's first outfit. They could have easily bought everything the little one needed. Unfortunately, they preferred to spend their money on alcohol.

I didn't know about it at the time and saw it as normal that we were poor and couldn't buy anything big.

When dad came home with the two of them, mom went straight to bed. She just left the little one to her own devices. But we were there. Dad showed me how to prepare a bottle and change the little one. It wasn't difficult, I had so much fun being there for Antonia. Our neighbor gave us a second-hand baby carriage so that I could regularly take my little sister out into the fresh air. I also affectionately called her my little rubber dummy, because babies don't have the strength to do anything themselves yet. I carefully held her little head when I had her in my arms. When she lay in my arms like that, I felt all the love in the world for the little mouse. But the situation at home didn't change. I had hoped that everything would get better when Toni was born, but instead I had the feeling that things were getting worse. My mother drank her alcohol, just like my father drank more and more, and I was there for the little one when I was at home. It was awful. I would have loved to go to my grandparents' house with Toni. But I wasn't allowed to.

My grandparents hadn't visited us for a long time and we never went to see them again. When I asked them why, I was told: "We broke off contact with them. I'm so fed up

with their meddling. They should stay where the pepper grows." Shocked, I stood in front of my mother.
"But mom, it's grandma and grandpa. I want to visit them."
"That's enough now, Cecilia. It's the way it is now and you get on with it. We'll be fine without her."
Those words stung. I was so hurt and desperate that I couldn't find any more words. Disappointed, I lay down on my mattress and cried. But it gave me hope that it was my mother's parents and you don't just break off contact like that, do you? My grandparents were such lovely people, why would they do something like that? Surely they were longing for me, weren't they? I was completely confused and no longer knew what to believe. But unfortunately my mother's stubbornness proved to be true. I was no longer allowed to see Grandma and Grandpa, I wasn't allowed to visit them and they stopped coming to see us.
My grandparents knew nothing about my mother's pregnancy and nothing about the birth of my little sister.

It hurt so terribly. I missed them so much.

One day I came back from our walk with Antonia, I always had to leave the baby carriage downstairs because I couldn't get it up the stairs. I carefully took her in my arms and walked to our apartment, the same thing every day, but I enjoyed it. My parents' voices could be heard outside that day. I rang the doorbell anxiously and Dad opened the door for me. His face was full of rage and he immediately stomped back into the kitchen. I went into the bedroom, undressed the little one and put her in her crib. Antonia was such a lovely baby. She didn't cry at that moment, so I went into the kitchen too. I was startled when I saw mom. She was sitting at the kitchen table and was totally drunk. Her hair, now very thin, was stringy and greasy, red spots covered her face, her eyes were in hollows and also had a reddish tinge. Dad reproached her loudly: "Stop your drinking! You have to look after your children, especially the baby!" he shouted at her.

She looked up at him weakly and slurred, "You do that, why me?"

"Because you're the mother, dammit! Children need their mother!"

"Your father too ... oh ... just leave me alone." She took the bottle from the table, which was almost empty, and drank the rest. By now I knew it was some cheap booze that Mom always drank. Dad got a beer from the fridge and emptied the bottle in one go. I was ten years old, my parents were drunk and there was a little baby in the bedroom who needed his parents. I looked after the little one as best I could. The only thing my parents did was check Antonia regularly, always hoping that her disability wasn't too pronounced. You could see it a bit on her face, but I didn't think it was a problem. She was completely normal to me and that's how I loved her. Antonia was my everything. It went on like that for the next few months. My parents argued loudly, fought, I almost always had to make my own food and I looked after Antonia pretty much on my own. I fervently hoped that my parents took good care of the little girl when I was at school.

It was shortly before my eleventh birthday, I came home from school and wanted to go to Toni immediately. But her bed was no longer in its place. I raced into the living room,

my parents were sitting on the sofa laughing. There was a half-full bottle of booze on the table. "Where's Toni?"
"In your room," laughed mom.
"What? But there's no more room," I said in shock. There was still some space, but I thought I would get a desk so I could do my homework in my room.
"Yes, that worked," Dad also laughed.
It was nice that they were so wonderfully cheerful. Nobody asked me how it was at school. Dad had promised me that if I helped with the baby, they would support me if I didn't understand something. Fiddlesticks, they didn't care about my performance, didn't ask if I was having problems learning. The only thing Dad had kept were envelopes for my exercise books and books, which I now finally had.

When mom changed or fed the little one, I always noticed that she showed no movement. She never smiled, cuddled or stroked Toni. She did her "work" mechanically. She then put her down in her crib without any words or love and that was the end of the "business" for her.
Dad cuddled her from time to time, but that also became less and less frequent.
I was now a regular customer at the library and obsessively read everything about children with Down's syndrome. Toni's signs could no longer be overlooked. Her head was very small and round, the back of her head was very flat, her eyes were wide apart, her nose was wide and her ears were very, very small. Her toes were also very strange, the big toe and the second toe were far apart. But Toni was still a very sweet little baby and I loved her. As much as I disliked her back then and didn't even want to look at her, I

loved her from the first time I saw her. Her eyes followed my every move. When I engaged with her, she always looked at me big. But I never saw her smile. When I asked why that was, my mother just said that "... she's not normal and won't ever be able to do anything ..."

The derogatory way she spoke about her little daughter was incomprehensible to me. I was still a child myself, but I knew that children needed love, affection and security. Even I longed for it, but I never got it. But it is all the more important for a small baby. Sometimes I even had to cry about my parents' coldness towards Toni. What would happen if she really did have mental deficits? I read so much about it that it was certain that Toni would never develop like a normal child, but she had to get all the support she could. Mom just said that there was still time. On the one hand I was stunned, but on the other I believed her, of course. After all, they were going to have tests with my sister, they would certainly get good advice there. I thought.

My everyday life now looked like this - school, baby, homework, going for walks with Toni and being shouted at or hit. The slightest thing was enough to make my mother's hand slip. I did everything I could to support her. I also needed help with my schoolwork, but after asking several times with refusals that I should see how I got on, I stopped asking and somehow struggled through my horrible everyday life on my own.

My mother almost only drank or sat and watched TV. She cooked for us less and less, did our laundry even less often and hardly ever cleaned. Our home became more and more chaotic.

Dirty dishes were piled up in the kitchen, flies and mold were swarming in the unwashed pots. In the living room there were empty and half-full bottles on the table, dirty glasses, the table was sticky everywhere. The ashtrays were overflowing and the floor was covered in stains.

The bedroom smelled extremely of alcohol, dirt and sweat. I can't tell you how long the bed linen had been up, disgusting. Dust and dirt everywhere you looked.

Our bathroom was also simply filthy. The toilet hadn't been cleaned for ages, the mirror was full of stains, the bathtub had a dark rim and the floor was dirty here too.

Except for my room, which was clean, I paid meticulous attention to cleanliness, as little Toni lived here with me and a baby needs cleanliness. The older I got, the worse I saw the extent of my parents' neglect and indifference.

At school, I thought about how I could change things and made a firm resolution to clean when I got home. Antonia was asleep, I went into the kitchen and washed the dishes. It took an hour, so much had accumulated and got dirty. Toni screamed, I ran to her, changed her and gave her the bottle. I picked up her blanket and took it into the kitchen, laying it carefully on the floor so that the little mouse could see me. I cleaned the worktop and the table, wiped the tiles above the sink and finally the floor. I looked around with satisfaction. It was nice as it was. But how was I supposed to tidy up the living room now? My parents were sitting there, they would just get upset if I walked around in front of the TV. I had just finished in the kitchen when my mom stumbled in, staggered to the fridge and scolded me: "There's nothing left, I'm going crazy..."

"Mom, I've cleaned everything here," I said proudly.

"Well, then you've finally done something useful and now you can go shopping. But take Antonia with you in the baby carriage, I want some peace and quiet."

"Actually, I wanted to clean the living room," I said miserably. Not a word of appreciation for my hard work came from her lips.

"When I say you're going shopping, you're going shopping." She was so loud again, Toni immediately started crying. That called my father to the scene.

"What's going on here again?" he rumbled immediately.

"Madame is supposed to go shopping and refuses, this useless brat."

I completely collapsed inside. Dad looked around: "Cecilia, have you cleaned this place?"

"Yes," I said quietly.

"Great," Dad praised me.

"I wanted to tidy up the living room, but Mom sent me shopping."

"You know what? We'll go together. You're not allowed to buy alcohol yet anyway, so we can bring everything else with us."

"But take the screamer with you!" Mom ordered.

"No, Toni stays here, you take care of it and when we come back, the living room will be clean," my father said.

"Nope ... a baby and cleaning? How am I supposed to manage that?"

"Your daughter also managed to clean up in the kitchen and had the baby with her, so don't be like that!"

So we set off and went shopping. Food, diapers, powdered milk, baby food, beer and schnapps. We had a little handcart that we always took to the discount store. Dad even bought me chocolate, which I got more than rarely because there was hardly ever any money for such "trinkets". On the way home, he put his arm around me: "You did a great job in the kitchen. You're my little princess." I smiled proudly at him and nodded. When we got home, we carried everything into the kitchen and put it away. Then came the big bang. Mom was sitting in the living room and it looked exactly as we had left it. She just lazed around and carried on drinking.

Dad snapped. "You miserable bastard ... I told you to clean up!"

"Do your own shit, you ass," she yelled back.

Now he'd had enough. Dad took her by the hair and dragged her off the couch and into the bedroom. Toni immediately started screaming, I took her in my arms and went into my room. I heard them both shouting, then there was the sound of clapping, over and over again. Fear spread through me. Toni screamed and screamed. I tried to calm her down, but it didn't help. I wonder what she had to put up with when I was at school?

After what felt like an eternity, it was finally quiet. I left my room listening. Toni had finally fallen asleep. The TV was on and I went into the living room: "Where's mom?"

"She's sleeping it off." I stood there dumbfounded when Dad suddenly jumped towards me. I immediately flinched. But he smiled at me: "You know what, princess? We're going to make something to eat and then we'll tidy up the living room together, or tidy up first and then eat?"

"You don't feel like cleaning up until we've eaten," I replied smart-assedly.

"OK, let's get to work." We had our hands full, but we got it done and it was clean. "Now you vacuum the floor and I'll cook us some spaghetti, what do you think?"

"Oh yes, delicious," I said happily.

Toni was with us at dinner and I fed her her porridge on the side. Even Dad fooled around with us. It could be so nice, why wasn't it always like that and why was mom never so relaxed and cheerful? I don't want to sugarcoat anything, my dad also drank a lot of alcohol, was often angry and hit my mother, but he could also have another side and I kept hoping that this time it would stay that way. The disappointment was never long in coming. After dinner, we washed the dishes together.

"So, you go and wash up and I'll get Toni ready for bed."

My little gummy was still awake when I came into our room that evening. She was fidgeting with her little arms. I took her into my bed with me. I was dog-tired from the exhausting day and fell asleep quickly. I woke up when Daddy took Toni out of my arms and put her in her crib. I wanted to go back to sleep, I was so tired. It was probably already the middle of the night. My eyes were already falling shut again when I realized that Dad was lying down with me. I immediately remembered the time he had stroked me between my legs. Since it never happened again, I had almost forgotten it. Now I immediately remembered it.

"Hey, my little princess, Daddy loves you so much." I didn't say anything. I didn't move an inch. My father reeked of alcohol. Toni's breathing was steady, she was fast asleep. Dad stroked my back, but his hand moved lower and lower. He stroked my bottom for a long time, then suddenly he said: "You know what? I have an idea, princess."

"I'm tired, Dad."

"Yes, then you can sleep even better, I'll give you a massage."

Anxiously, I replied: "Not today Dad, I'm really dead tired."

"So what? You don't have to do anything, just enjoy, so get undressed and lie on your stomach. I'll give you a massage ..."

What should I do? I undressed and lay on my stomach. My feeling was bad.

He massaged my shoulders and my back and it felt really good. I slowly relaxed. It really was nice, he was right.

"I've brought some cream, it'll work even better and be even more comfortable for you." I believed him. Dad spread the cream on my back and massaged me. It was actually very pleasant until he got to my bottom. I was still relaxed, but he didn't just massage my bottom from the outside, no, his fingers also went into my little crack and he rubbed and rubbed. It started to hurt. His fingers moved further and further forward, right up to my most intimate area. He took some new cream and massaged me between my legs: "Turn on your back, princess!" I obeyed, rigid with fear. By now I was paralyzed. He took off his pyjama bottoms, spread cream on my upper body and massaged my stomach and chest. He lingered for a long time. I was still a child, there was almost nothing there yet. But he acted as if I already had breasts.

"You are so beautifully tender," Dad breathed.

But his hand didn't stay there, it moved between my legs. Again he put new cream on his fingers and pushed a finger inside me. This sudden pain was terrible. It hurt so much!!! But I didn't make a sound. I lay there still and stiff. He moved his finger back and forth inside me. My little vagina was burning like fire, I didn't scream, I was too scared, it paralyzed me completely, but I whimpered and sobbed quietly to myself. Tears ran down my face. Dad's fingers got faster and faster, he moaned louder and louder. I saw that he was rubbing his penis faster and faster with his other hand. I squeezed my eyes shut tightly, not wanting to look. He let out a loud groan and it was finally over.

Dad leaned over to me: "Hey, my little princess, that was really nice, wasn't it?" I looked at him timidly under a veil of tears, but he just laughed: "You'll see, you'll like it one day too. That's how you show that you love each other. But don't you dare say a word to anyone and a disaster will happen here!" He was finally gone. I pulled my blanket up to my chin and cried unrestrainedly for an eternity. Didn't he see my tears? Didn't he realize that I didn't want what he was doing? If people showed love like that, why couldn't I say anything to anyone? I knew exactly what my father was doing to me was wrong. I was no longer a little baby. From that day on, my father came at night at least twice a week and pleasured me. It hurt indescribably every time.

Did I love him? Yes, I did. During the day, when he was nice, joked around with me and spent time with me and Toni, I loved him like you can only love your father. At night, when he came to me, I hated his guts. I didn't believe his fairy tale about love. If you love each other, you don't hurt each other. I was convinced of that. When he was drunk, he would shout or hit my mother, I don't think I loved or hated him then, there was only the feeling of fear. I withdrew more and more from everything. Nobody took any notice of me at school and at home I tried to avoid my parents, which I rarely succeeded in doing. My mother always found a reason to scold me or hit me.

She thought I was now old enough to do my own laundry in the washing machine. She showed me how to use it once and that was it. But I wasn't so stupid and washed Toni's clothes too. I carefully folded everything after drying and put it away in the cupboard. Once, however, I used too much washing powder and the laundry just didn't get free of it. The fabric was sticky and hard. I called my mother and showed her the mess. Today I know that you would have just switched on the rinse program again and then it would have been fine. Not so my mother.

"You rare stupid piece, you really are too stupid for

anything. I showed you," she roared, threw the laundry into the bathtub and her blows were already raining down on me. She beat me ruthlessly everywhere. Her hands were not enough for her. She took a wet piece of laundry and hit my head and back with it. She also hit me in the face with it, my lip burst open and blood streamed down my face. It hurt so damn much. All of a sudden she stopped hitting me. I heard Toni crying, but I couldn't get to her like that. "Clean yourself up and then rinse the laundry here in the bath and hang it up!" She was gone. When I looked at myself in the mirror, I was extremely scared. My lip was bleeding and swelling, I had red spots everywhere that were guaranteed to turn blue. On my back, face and neck. I washed my face briefly, ignored my pain as best I could and rinsed the laundry under running water. When I had finished everything, I wanted to go to my room. Dad crossed my path and looked at me, startled. "What's happened to you?" I didn't say a word. "Was that your mother?" I still didn't say anything. "Cecilia, I asked you a question!" Now I nodded and went straight to my room. My parents shouted angrily at each other. At dinner, my mother said to me: "You're not going to school for a week." Of course, I didn't say anything back, although I didn't mind not having to go to school either. On the contrary, I was quite happy about it despite my pain. She couldn't let me go to school the way she'd beaten me up.

It was summer again and my sister now had a sports car so I could take her for a walk. Her Down syndrome could no longer be overlooked. But I wasn't ashamed of her. On the contrary, I was proud of my little sister. I was walking down

our street when children from my class crossed our path.
"Oh, Stinkie's going for a walk. Are you babysitting?" I didn't want to respond, but they wouldn't let us pass.
"Leave me alone, I want to go for a walk with my sister," I said bravely. When they looked at Toni, their eyes widened, then they laughed: "That's your sister? A mongoose? ... a spaz? ... Well, that suits you ..." They laughed and Toni laughed with them. The little girl didn't understand that the others were angry with us. She thought they were laughing with us and just did the same. A girl, she was a bit older, I didn't know her, approached Toni and stroked her cheek: "Hey, what's your name? Spasti? Goggle-eyed? Droolhead?" I slapped her hand away and kept walking. I could hear a lot of cheering. How can you be so mean? Tears streamed down my face. I wondered what would become of my little sister. I can't be there for her forever. At some point I'll have to do an apprenticeship, go to work and maybe I'll have a family of my own. Will Toni always be teased or worse?

From that day onwards, I wasn't just Stinkie at school, I was the Mongo sister, the one with the spaz appendage from the Assi family. There were lots of children from socially disadvantaged families in my class, but no one was as neglected as me. As I withdrew more and more, no longer mentally participated in lessons at all and bruises were noticed during PE lessons, my class teacher spoke to me after class:
"Cecilia, is everything all right with you? You've always been a very quiet student, but now you're not cooperating at all. Your performance is plummeting." I shrugged my

shoulders, what could I say? That my mother beats me or shouts at me, that my father abuses me? Never.

"I take care of my sister a lot," it wasn't even a lie.

"As far as I know, your parents are both at home. Don't get me wrong, it's great that you're looking after your little sister, but your parents have to take on the main responsibility."

"They do," I claimed.

"Then why are you so quiet and so weak in terms of performance? I know you're not stupid. You could do it easily if you put your mind to it."

No, now I was in tears too. What was I supposed to do? I didn't even have a desk so I could work for school in peace. What's more, I was almost entirely made up of fear. Fear of being teased at school, of being ostracized by others and fear at home in front of my father and mother. I would have liked to say: 'Just come and have a look around and maybe you'll see what's going on here'.

"OK, Cecilia, let's do it this way: I'll give you a letter for your parents saying that I'd like to speak to them with you on Wednesday at 2 pm. Please ask them to come to school."

"No, don't do that. I'll make an effort, I promise."

"But Cecilia, that's not a bad thing. I just want to have a chat with you and your parents. I won't put you on the spot, I promise you that." I had no choice but to take the letter and go home. Full of fear, I handed the letter to my father.

"Why should we come to school? Have you done something wrong?" he asked me.

"No, I didn't," I managed to get out.

"Beate, we're supposed to come to school on Wednesday for a talk."

"Nooo forget it ... I'm not going to that school. Go on your own, it's your PRINCESS and not mine." Did she know about the nights when Daddy came to see me or why did she emphasize the word 'princess' so much?
"Aren't you interested in what's going on with Cecilia at school?"
"Nope, not in the slightest." My God, how can someone like that call themselves a 'mother'?

I was terrified of my father that Wednesday. He was there on time. Luckily he was at least shaved, which was very rare. He let himself go completely at home. That's how he always smelled - of alcohol, old sweat and unwashed. Today he looked quite acceptable. The conversation with my teacher didn't last long. My father promised to pay more attention to my performance and to help me with my homework. When I asked him why he hadn't intervened sooner with all the bad grades, he shrugged his shoulders. "Well, Cecilia is slowly entering puberty or is already in the middle of it, so we didn't really think anything of it. Things are getting better, we'll take care of it." This farce was finally over. He didn't say a word to me on the way home. But as soon as we got home, it started: "Are you really too stupid to pay attention at school and do your homework properly? Man, man, man. You're not a little baby anymore," he rumbled at me. What was I supposed to say? That I couldn't sleep at night for fear of him coming to me again? That I could never do my homework in peace because I had no place to retreat to and had to work at the kitchen table instead? When I was in my mother's way, I had to get out of there? That I had to look after my little sister? That I had to clean? That I had to do my own laundry? Should I list all that? Yes, I would have loved to, but of course I didn't dare. My mother just sat there and grinned: "Stupid stays stupid." What had I done to her to make her despise me so much?

Sadly, I went into my room, took my sister out of her bed and played with her. She was almost always lying in her bed when I wasn't there. My mother only did the bare minimum, Dad sometimes spent time with her, but this was still very rare. With my mother, I sometimes even had the feeling that she was disgusted by Toni, her own daughter. Yes, the little girl drooled uncontrollably, saliva was always running out of her mouth, but I still loved her, why couldn't my mother do that? I couldn't really play with her yet either. She couldn't crawl or walk yet. Apart from "there..." and "ma ..." came nothing from the little mouse. Nevertheless, I took her onto my lap and showed her books that I had brought for her from the library. I explained every picture, every animal and read her fairy tales. She always smiled so sweetly at me. But more and more often I noticed that as soon as she saw my mother, she started to cry violently. Sometimes it was so bad that she got the hiccups from crying. When my father was around her, I noticed that she could sense exactly whether he was in a good or bad mood. Then she was either very quiet and anxious, or she was hyper and made funny noises, which was never a word or anything like that. But then you could tell that she was just fine. After I had read her a fairy tale, I told her that I was doing badly at school.

"Oh my Tonichen, I don't enjoy school at all and I don't like it here at home either. I'd love to run away, but I can't leave you here. The best thing would be for us both to live with grandma and grandpa. We'd have a really nice time there. They are so loving. Unfortunately, we can't go there, not even for a visit. I promise you, when I'm old enough and earn some money, the two of us will leave here. I'll never leave you alone." I hugged my little sister tightly and cried. Cried and cried. I couldn't stop. It was as if everything collapsed on top of me. I poured out all my despair and grief. My sister's shirt was all wet afterwards and I quickly put a fresh one on her so that my mother couldn't complain again. Toni was very quiet and let me cry. She let herself be pressed against me and waited. Very unusual for such a small child, but that's how my little Toni was. Very sensitive and compassionate. As small as she was, she felt more than we all thought. She was two years old. She couldn't walk yet. Crawling was very slow. She slowly pulled herself up on pieces of furniture, stood on wobbly legs for a few seconds and then fell over again and laughed. It was actually just indefinable sounds and grins that she made. Antonia couldn't speak a word yet. I practiced with her incessantly, singing songs to her and fooling around.

And I was to be rewarded. Shortly after her third birthday, Toni was able to walk. She pulled herself up by the kitchen chair, stood there wobbly, I squatted down and spread my arms out: "Come on, Toni, I dare you," I laughed at her. And she came. Still a little unsure, but she walked. I was proud of the mouse. I took her firmly in my arms, put her down and backed away from her a little. Again I asked her to come to me. She did, Toni became more and more secure on her little legs. Beaming with joy, I took her in my arms and ran with her to my parents in the living room.

"Mom, Dad ... look," I was so excited that I let Toni stand on her little feet, moved a little further away from her and spread my arms out. Laughing, she ran into my arms. I looked proudly at my parents. Dad smiled and Mom said: "Well, it's about time."
Dad came over to us and put his arms around us both. "Well done, you two." I looked at my mother from the side and she just rolled her eyes.

Today I know, and the fact is incredible, that Toni would have needed physiotherapy. Exercises at home would have been so important. Children with Down's syndrome need to be supported. But my parents didn't care. UNBELIEVABLE! Sure, I read a lot about this disease, but the support provided by physiotherapy apparently escaped me.
But I kept my promise: I was always there for her, giving her as much affection, love and, above all, time as I could. Toni was such a loving and grateful child, but she was also very stubborn. What she didn't want, she didn't want. Not a chance. Since she could now walk and she wanted something, she went and got it. I was only after her. But I enjoyed it. Antonia always made unintelligible noises, no matter what she did, but over time I learned what she meant. If you spent time with her, you soon understood. But my parents didn't seem to be interested. They left her to her own devices or to me. Of course they went to check-ups, they had to, otherwise the youth welfare office would be on the mat, but unfortunately they only did what they had to, nothing more. It was clear to me that I would go through hell for Antonia. I would do everything I could to protect her and always be there for her. I felt so sorry that she had no loving

parents to give her love and security.

I was now fourteen years old, Toni was five. She still couldn't speak properly. Some children with this illness only really speak coherently and clearly at the age of eleven or thirteen. But I didn't want to believe that and practiced and practiced with her. But it was to no avail. This fact made me very sad, but I never lost heart and never gave up.

It was Saturday. I had done my usual chores, washed the laundry, cleaned my room and washed the dishes. After dinner, I got Toni ready for bed and lay down on my bed. For quite some time, I just called "Good night" into the living room and disappeared. I hoped for a kiss at night so often when I went to my parents' house with the little one, but it never happened. As I said before, I think my mother was even disgusted by her. Today I sang "Good evening, good night..." to her and she fell asleep very quickly. I closed my eyes and daydreamed. I heard HIM and my heart immediately started racing. No, please don't!
He came into my room, went to Toni's bed and saw that she was fast asleep.
"You're not even ready for bed yet," my father said.
"It's not that late, I'm not a baby anymore," I replied nonchalantly.
"That's right, you're slowly becoming a young lady. But you'll still be my little princess. We're going to make ourselves comfortable now. Mom is sleeping it off and Toni is also in dreamland. Time for the two of us." I knew what I had to do, undress and lie on my stomach so that Daddy could 'massage' me. Without a word, I did what I had to do. My heart was racing, my hands were shaking as I undressed. My father watched me greedily. But today he

wanted me to lie on my back. He looked at me longer and much more greedily than usual. That scared me even more. He smeared cream on my chest and massaged it for a long time. "Something's really growing there. You're so tender and firm, my little princess." He stood up briefly and took off his pants and shorts. He smelled so unpleasant that I had to pull myself together not to throw up. As he sat down next to me, he continued to massage my little chest, moving over my stomach and down between my legs. He squatted on his knees next to me and massaged his penis. His fingers hurt me incredibly. I closed my eyes and hoped it would pass quickly. Today I was going to be wrong. It never went by quickly, for me it was always an endless eternity. But today was different. "I love you," I heard him breathe. At his words, he lay on top of me. I felt his hard thing nudging my vagina, more and more demanding. I lay there stiff as a board, he reached for the cream jar, applied a lot of cream underneath and thrust. He penetrated me so brutally that I screamed. I couldn't help it. He put a hand over my mouth: "Shut up ... think of Toni ...", that was all he needed to say. For God's sake, I'd forgotten all about the little girl. The pain was just too overwhelming. It hurt so much that I couldn't help it. It moved back and forth on and inside me. It tore me to pieces. Into a thousand pieces. How can a person be so cruel? And then his own father!!! Yes, he was my stepfather, but did it change the fact that he wasn't allowed to do this? As I couldn't stop myself from screaming, Toni woke up and screamed because I was screaming. She cried like crazy. But that didn't bother my father. He did his "business" until he was finished, just before his climax he let go of me and squirted the disgusting stuff on my stomach. He got off me, got dressed and stroked his little daughter's head. He said to me: "That was good. I love your innocent screaming," he grinned and left. He loved my pain? He had raped me, that's all it was and he loved that? That he hurt me so much? Wasn't he afraid that my mother would be woken up by my screaming?

I was lying on my bed and didn't know what to do with myself because of the pain. It throbbed relentlessly between my legs and the feeling of a million pins and needles and burning was indescribable. My body felt like an open wound. I lay there for a long time, frozen in pain. Slowly my fingers felt their way to the worst painful spot, felt something slippery, looked at my fingers and was scared to death - blood. My fingers were red. I struggled to sit up and saw that my sheets were also covered in it. What had he done to me? Was I injured? Then the scales fell from my eyes - my father had taken my virginity, that much I already knew at my age. But I was definitely hurt too, the blood was just too much. I had once read that you bleed a little when you take a girl's virginity. This wasn't just a little. I fell back onto my pillow in despair. The urgent need to wash myself grew ever greater. To wash HIM off. But I didn't dare. Could I even walk with the pain? I was terrified. Afraid of meeting him again tonight and afraid of running. Now my bladder was also making itself heard, this need was becoming more and more intense. 'God, what should I do? I couldn't get up, I just couldn't. So I let it go. Yes, I urinated in bed.

I was so lost in my fear, pain and despair that I didn't notice that my little sister was still crying. I looked at her, she was standing in her crib, looking at me and crying heartbreakingly. I took my pyjama top, which was lying next to my bed, and made a makeshift wipe of the disgusting stuff on my stomach.

Didn't my mother hear Toni scream? No, she didn't. The alcohol intoxication was stronger. Did my father hear it? Yes, he even knew, but he had to sleep off the effort of satisfying me.

"Toni, lie down Mouse, you need to sleep," I tried to persuade her quietly. But she didn't calm down. Her little face was all puffy from crying, snot and saliva were running down her chin and over her pyjamas, everything was already wet. I HAD to get up. For her sake. And I did. Oh God, the burning pain. When I finally stood up, I looked down at myself. Blood was running down my thighs. No matter, Toni was more important now. Slowly, I managed to take one step in front of the other. I finally reached her, our room was very small. I lifted the little crying mouse out of her crib, hugged her tightly to my chest and sat down on my bed for the night. At that moment, I forgot about the blood on my legs and in my bed. Antonia noticed it immediately. She stopped crying abruptly and stared at the blood stain on my sheets. Her gaze was fixed on it. She didn't move. Just stared at it. What goes on in a small child at a time like that? I kept trying to calm her down with soothing words.

"Cecilia has had a boo-boo, Toni. It's not bad, it's all right now." But she seemed to be far away from me. She kept staring at that damn blood. It was awful and I was getting more and more perplexed. We sat there for a long time until she finally looked at me when I spoke. Not a sound escaped her lips.

"I'll put you in your bed now and then I'll make my bed. If you're really quiet, I'll bring you to me and we'll both fall asleep together, okay?" Toni just looked at me, she didn't react at all. I didn't know, was it the shock of what she had seen? What had she noticed when my father was here or was it because of her disability? Had my screaming scared her? I felt so guilty. As soon as I had put the little girl to bed, I turned away from her to go to my wardrobe. In a flash, she pulled herself to her feet, stood by the bars and started crying loudly again. She had to go through this now. I wanted a fresh bed, it didn't take that long. Antonia really started to scream. "Toni, be quiet," I begged her. To no avail.

Suddenly the door flew open and my mother was standing in the room:

"What kind of circus is going on here, you snotty brats? You're waking up the whole neighborhood," she shouted at us. Furious, she went to the crib, roughly picked up her little daughter and scolded her: "Be quiet and stop shouting, otherwise you'll have a reason to shout!" It had the effect of making my little sister scream even louder. My mother looked at me, glanced at my bed sheet: "What's happened to you?" she whined at me. At that moment, I couldn't take any more. I literally collapsed inside, my legs started to shake and tears streamed down my face.

"Stop crying! You got your period. That's not the end of it. I'll give you pads and then it's fine. That's how it is with us girls." My mother didn't shout at me now. She was almost calm. In fact, she was smiling at me. Antonia was still on her arm and screaming. "I'll get you some pads," they were both gone. Back again, my mother threw me sanitary towels

and put the little girl in her bed.
"Go wash yourself, I'll do this!" What was wrong with her? The way she was, I would have loved to throw myself into her arms and tell her everything. No, I hadn't started my period. I'd been having them for six months. My mother just hadn't noticed that I was using her pads. She was too preoccupied with herself and her alcohol to notice anything so important about me.
Didn't she want to see what was actually going on here?

But it was strange that she was nice by her standards and helped me in the middle of the night. Incredibly slowly, I trotted into the bathroom and washed off the blood and its disgusting stuff. I didn't dare "waste" a lot of water in the middle of the night. She had followed me unnoticed: "It would be better if you took a bath." Oh, how gracious, of course I was pleased. Too happy too soon. The bath water made my vagina burn even more. It was just as bad on the toilet afterwards. It burned and burned. A nest of embers between my legs. After I was finally finished and had changed into fresh clothes, I went back and lay down.
"Can you give me Toni?"
"Why? She should stop screaming and go to sleep."
"She calms down in bed with me."
"Is that so? Yes, well then ..."
So she put the crying child in my arms. On the way out, she warned: "I hope it's finally quiet now!"
"Yes, mom, thank you for your help."
She was gone. After Antonia had calmed down a bit, I gave her something to drink, wiped her face, so she calmed down and then finally fell asleep. The little girl was exhausted. It

was a sleepless night for me. Fortunately, I didn't have to go to school the next day.

My pain was just as bad in the morning as it had been during the night. Still, it didn't help, I had to get up, Antonia was awake. She needed a fresh diaper and fresh clothes. There was still absolute silence in the apartment. My parents were sound asleep. When I had the little one ready, I made her something to eat, fed her and didn't eat anything myself. I didn't get a single bite down. I just drank a glass of tap water. Just as I was about to leave the kitchen, my father came in. My heart immediately went into overdrive. "You're really pale today," he whispered, winking at me with one eye. Then my mother came in too. She immediately said: "Jens, your daughter got her period tonight." My father looked at me questioningly. After all, he knew about it and he was fully aware that I hadn't had my period last night. But he just said: "Oh, that's why she's so pale, I was wondering." Turning to me, he just said: "Well then, you're slowly becoming a young woman. Make sure you don't get pregnant." He laughed and made coffee. I couldn't take it anymore.
"Take Antonia out into the fresh air and you'll feel better faster," my mother demanded.
"No, I can't. Everything hurts."
She was already getting impatient again: "Cecilia, you can go out into the fresh air for a bit of period pain. It's not that bad. Take a tablet and that's it. Otherwise you'll be in real pain. It's enough that I've been up all night, now don't go crazy and make yourself look like a poor period victim." Her voice got louder and louder.

"I'd rather lie down again," I protested weakly.

"Nothing, you take your sister now and go out with her. I need my peace and quiet too!" she scolded. She needed her rest? From what?

Toni sat in her little chair, stretched her little arms forward and opened and closed her little hands alternately. That was the sign for me that she wanted to come to me. In the meantime, I was the mom and not the child in this family. I was the sex object for my father and the cleaner and babysitter for my mother.

When I was out in the fresh air with my little sister, I was thinking about her. What would she actually become one day? Will she go to school? Can she learn? Does she understand? These thoughts made me very sad. I made up my mind to ask my parents about it. The answer I got later was outrageous: "Don't worry about it, we'll sort it out. She's too stupid to understand anything anyway ... we'll have to go to a counseling center, they'll take care of it ..."

Why was there no kindergarten for Toni? I didn't ask anymore.

My father left me alone for two weeks. But I still couldn't sleep properly at night. Every day I was afraid he would come to me and hurt me. But maybe he was now afraid or had lost the desire to abuse me? I was wrong. He opened the door very quietly that night, put his index finger to his lips and sat down next to me.

"Shall we get really cozy again?" Why did he ask me that? As if he cared what I thought. Unconsciously, I pulled the blanket over my head. He pulled it down: "Don't act like that now, is it so bad to show me that you love me? You do love me, don't you?" I nodded timidly. Fear paralyzed me once again.

"I won't hurt you, little princess. Look, I've brought something that won't hurt you." He held out a small piece of plastic to me, a small dildo. Holy shit! Not that too.

"Take your clothes off! I'll take care of the rest." Again he applied cream all over me, especially my pubic area. He switched this thing on and inserted it into my vagina. It buzzed slightly and he slowly pushed it back and forth. What can I say? This feeling was almost 'nice'. NO! That can't be right, what is it now? It's not supposed to be nice!!! But I couldn't help it, a few moaning sounds escaped me.

"Yes, you like that, Princess. That's it." He also began to moan and rubbed his penis.

"Take the dildo in your own hand, satisfy yourself with it and suck my thing at the same time."

What should I do? Never!

"Go on, he's just waiting for you." He pulled me onto my knees, put the plastic thing back inside me and guided my hand so that I had to hold the dildo. He roughly grabbed the back of my neck and pushed me down so that I had his disgusting thing right in front of my mouth. The stench! Disgusting! "Open your mouth, princess!"

I opened my mouth and took him in. He pushed my head down and pulled it up, always alternating. The feeling in my vagina was now just painful. "Use your tongue and suck nicely ... yes ... that's it ..." I made every effort to make sure it was over quickly. I let go of the dildo, it was now too painful.

When he climaxed, this disgusting stuff squirted into my mouth: "Swallow princess," he laughed. That was the end of it. I threw up in the middle of his disgusting thing. I was ready for anything, even a beating for throwing up. Nothing of the sort happened. He laughed: "At least this way you can't get pregnant, sweetie" and left. I had to remake my bed again. I did this as quietly as I could. Luckily, my sister was fast asleep. That night I threw up a lot, I spent ages washing myself and brushing my teeth until there was blood. It was disgusting what he did to me. What else was to come?

When I was back in bed, I couldn't get my behavior out of my head. Why did I like it with the dildo at the beginning? That couldn't be right. Of course, I now know that it was a completely normal, biological process that had nothing to do with pleasure at all. I was stimulated without pain and my body reacted. But this son of a bitch of a father told himself that I thought it was great and that there was nothing better for me. How sick!!!

Christmas was just around the corner. It was something special at home, if you could call it that. My father always insisted on having a Christmas tree, which he meticulously decorated himself. This year, Antonia and I were allowed to help. However, my little sister's motor skills were still limited, so I took her in my arms, put the bauble in her hand and guided her little hands until the bauble was hanging on the tree. That was fun for her. When my father switched on the fairy lights, she was beaming all over her face. My mother couldn't cook, she only ever had bread or tinned ready meals. My father cooked at Christmas and he was good at it. We didn't have Christmas goose or roast duck. No, that was far too expensive, we had cheap meat, but he could really make something out of it, I had to give him that. There was a small Advent wreath on the living room table. But we didn't sing Christmas carols together or play together. After dinner, everyone got a small present. That year I got a book about rare natural phenomena and natural wonders. I was interested in that. My sister got a small, cheap doll, at least it was something. My parents gave each other alcohol. And what else? I would have been happy with some clothes too. I didn't have any presents, I never had any money. Although I missed my grandparents every day and longed for them, Christmas was the worst. Unfortunately, I couldn't talk to anyone about it. Contact had been broken off, my mother wanted it that way and there was nothing I could do about it.

However, when I noticed that my parents were getting drunker and drunker the later it got, I retired with Toni. I played with her for a bit, then we went to bed. I lay awake for a long time when sleep finally overcame me. I woke up to my father standing in front of me by the bed.

"Shhh," he didn't say any more at first, sat down next to me and held out a package. "This is just for you, princess. Unwrap it!" he smiled. I was happy, but I also had a bad feeling. I anxiously took the package, revealing a pair of red panties and a red lace bra. What was that all about?

"I'd love for you to put it on and show me how it looks on you." I stared at him, stunned. "That wasn't a request! Go on, you ungrateful thing. I want to make you happy and you look like a stuck calf." Great pleasure. It was just his joke. When I had the stuff on, I wanted to crawl into a corner, I was so ashamed. My father pulled me onto his lap and looked at me greedily. He could no longer keep his hands to himself. He groped me all over. "Lie down, I'll spoil you a little." I had no choice.

Since he pushed the dildo in me, he came regularly. As it didn't hurt, I put up with it. His thing in my mouth was disgusting and disgusting. He always insisted on it now. I learned to deal with the nausea. I no longer had to throw up. Maybe he took that to mean that I liked it too. However, the dildos got bigger and bigger over time. I never screamed again, I didn't want Antonia to notice or wake up. He knew exactly how much I loved my sister and didn't make any more noise for her sake. He stroked my bottom for a particularly long time today, applying cream. Especially a lot between my buttocks. I lay there quietly and suddenly a pain went through me that couldn't be described. Worse than anything he had ever done to me before. In pain and desperation, I bit into my pillow and clawed at the sheets. Just don't scream! But I couldn't stand it. I screamed like a wounded animal. It hurt like hell. I wanted to turn away, to push him off me, but he held me by the waist. I was small and petite for my age, Dad was big and had hands like cake tins. I didn't stand a chance. Why didn't my mother hear me? He finally pulled out of me, rubbing his disgusting thing himself until he climaxed. My little sister woke up and cried, of course.

"It's a madhouse here, you stupid brats, your shouting," he scolded and disappeared. I had to let Toni cry because I couldn't move. I was so shocked I could hardly bear the pain. Like an old granny, I dragged myself bent over into the bathroom, took a cloth and washed myself. I threw those stupid red underwear in the bin in disgust, my mother never looked. The garbage wasn't her job, it was mine. I put on my pyjamas and hobbled back. I had to take care of my sister. She stared at my bed and cried. She noticed more than I would have liked. Why couldn't my father be aware of this?

There was never enough money at home. Healthy food - not a thing. Why did he have the money for the dildos and underwear? He was constantly bringing in something else that disgusted and repelled me every time. Underwear with openings, bras with openings, lace shirts, long stockings and so on and so forth.

There was no stopping my father now. He came to me regularly and abused me in all sorts of ways. I can't describe everything he did to me. I have no words for it, I feel incredibly ashamed and disgusted. He was meticulous about using condoms.

I finally had my own apartment key, which my father gave

me as a reward for his rape of me one night. So I no longer had to ring the doorbell. It was a Wednesday when I got home. As usual, I rushed to my little sister, greeted her and started my cleaning work. I had just finished when the doorbell rang. I opened it and a woman and a man stood in front of me: "Hello, you must be Cecilia? Are your parents in?" I called my parents. My father came:
"Hello, Mr. E ... , we're from the youth welfare office and would like to have a look around."
"Please what? From the youth welfare office? Why?"
"Can we discuss this inside?"
"Make an appointment with us and then come back." Dad wanted to throw the door shut again, but the man quickly put his foot between them.
"We don't have to register. Please let us in, otherwise we'll have to come back with the police!" Fortunately, he spoke quietly. I was already ashamed of myself.
Thank goodness I had tidied up and even taken the empty bottles to the container. My mother was as good as new, she even offered fresh coffee.
"We have received information that your children lack some things and that there are often cries from your home. In addition, Cecilia's lack of concentration, severe pallor and bruises have been noticed at school. Of course, we have to look into this." After a short pause, the lady continued: "We would like to have a look around your home and also speak to the children."
My father had now also composed himself: "Our little daughter has Down's syndrome, she can't talk to you."
"We'll manage," came from the man in a firm voice.
Although I had fortunately tidied up, the two of them

looked at our apartment in disgust. After they had inspected everything, they asked me to go into my room with them and talk. I was afraid of saying the wrong thing. Or should I just tell them everything? For God's sake, never. I was far too ashamed for that. They asked me all sorts of questions. What I ate at school, what my daily routine was like at home and, above all, where did the bruises come from? I lied to them about the typical excuses of falling down the stairs, bike accidents, running into the door. I also told them that I was often pinched by the other children. They were satisfied with that, but promised to talk to the teachers about it. "No, I don't want that, then I'll be the tattletale and it'll be even worse. I'll soon have finished school."
"So you don't want that?"
I shook my head. When asked how my parents treated me, I replied: "Quite normal."
"But why are there so many screams coming from your apartment, especially at night?" I had to hold back my tears at this question. "My sister is ill and she often just screams at night."
"But then your parents are comforting the little girl?"
"Yes," I lied cheekily to her face.
"Your room is very small, where do you do your homework?"
"In the kitchen."
"Okay, Cecilia, that's it for us for now."
We went back to the living room. The woman took my little sister in her arms: "You're such a sweetie. Where are your mom and dad?"
Toni first looked at mom and then at my father. When she looked at him, she started to cry.

"Oh dear ... you don't have to cry, little darling, it's all right," she tried to reassure the little girl. I immediately jumped up and took my sister from her.

The conclusion of this visit was that my parents had to go for a consultation on how to proceed with Antonia in terms of support and later with school. They also had to make sure that I had a place to retreat to where I could work on my schoolwork. They had a lot to say. Where was the space supposed to come from? My parents were also supposed to provide healthy food. A look in the fridge revealed that we didn't have any fresh fruit and vegetables, and there was no cheese either. I also had the feeling that they weren't buying the excuse of my classmates' tricks. There was plenty of alcohol in the fridge.

"Okay, Mr. and Mrs. E., that's it from our side for now. We'll come back in a few months and see if you've been able to implement everything we complained about. You can contact us at any time if you need support." They said a friendly goodbye and left. My parents breathed a sigh of relief.

"We managed that well. You kids too. It was great how we stuck together," said Dad happily. I was anything but happy. I was far too annoyed with myself. I wish I'd told him everything.

"What if something else comes from them?" I asked uncertainly.

"Oh, what else is there to come? Definitely not. They said they'd be back in a few months. It's all good," laughed Dad. My parents were so relieved that they immediately opened their bottles. Where did they get their security from? Maybe the youth welfare office took some steps? I never got a desk and the people from the youth welfare office never showed up at our house again. But one thing had changed. My father now always insisted on fruit and vegetables when we went shopping. Nothing special, cheap apples, green cucumber, cheese and some sausage. Now I finally had a snack at school. Apart from that, it was business as usual. I had to do the laundry, wash the dishes and, more recently, clean the bathroom, and I also had my school work to do on the side. I loved looking after my sister.

I thought more and more about finishing school. It was clear to me that this, combined with a good education, was the only way out of this hell. This goal became more and more firmly established and it gave me strength.

My little sister had been attending an institution for mentally handicapped children for three months. She was still wearing diapers and couldn't speak yet either. Only syllables came out of her little mouth. At least her motor skills had improved and I practiced and spent as much time with her as I could. There were trained staff at the facility, so she was able to do more and more and was learning. This was proof that she simply had to be encouraged. My parents didn't care, but I did. My sister was my everything and I was incredibly happy about every progress she made. Yes, I was proud of my little Antonia.
During the day I did my chores, at night I studied or had to satisfy my father. I never knew what it was like to sleep in. I was tired and exhausted all the time, but I never gave up. My motto was to keep going and fight.

I was sitting in the kitchen doing my homework. Antonia was asleep and my parents were busy watching TV and drinking alcohol in the living room. I still wanted to learn school material, I still had my goal of a good degree firmly in mind. I was determined to achieve this. My performance improved despite all the bad circumstances at home.

I was so engrossed in my English book that I only noticed my mother when she said to me: "What are you doing here?"

"Study, Mom."

She was drunk because she was slurring her words.

"I'm going to bed ... I have a headache, so no more noise from your room tonight!"

Yes, the madam needed her rest. She was gone. Antonia played in our room, she could keep herself busy from time to time.

About an hour later, HE came into the kitchen:

"Hey, my little princess, are you still busy?" He was drunk too. I just nodded. My father pretended to be interested in what I was learning. I felt an unpleasant tingling sensation. I wanted to be alone and learn. I always felt anxious in his presence. That evening was no exception. He suddenly stood behind me, reached forward to my breasts and stroked them. I fended off his hands, but I hadn't reckoned with his obsession. "Now, now, now, princess, don't be so coy."

"Dad, I have to study," I tried miserably to protest, knowing that it wouldn't do any good anyway. He was still standing behind my chair, stroking me. I sat rigidly and stiffly in my seat. He gently pulled me up and now I was standing in front of him. He reached into my pants, wandered into my briefs and stuck first one, then another finger inside me. I held very still. 'Please, let it pass quickly. When he took his fingers off me, I thought it was over. No, he opened my pants, pulled them down with my panties and lifted me up, saying, "Wrap your legs around me!" I did, he put me down on the table, spat in his hands and rubbed them between my legs. He pushed me backwards onto the table and penetrated me. For the first time, he didn't rape me in my room, but in the middle of the kitchen table. Next to us were my school things, a teenager's school books, while she was being raped by her father! He kept moaning: "Yes, that's good princess, you like that, I know." Was he not afraid that my mother could suddenly be in the kitchen? Was he sure that she was so drunk that she was really fast asleep? There was really no other explanation. My father was sure that she wouldn't turn up. He hurt me beyond description. I was always sore between my legs, so the penetration hurt terribly over and over and over again, it could never really heal. Abuse and rape were part of my everyday life. I had no choice but to accept it. What else could I have done? Sure, more than once I thought about simply running away. But then I would have to leave Toni behind, and I couldn't do that. She only had me to give her love and take care of her. My parents didn't encourage her in the slightest.

"They're already doing it at the crazy school," my mother would say snidely when I asked her to look after Toni.

"Mom, why don't you play with Antonia, the little one needs you."

"She doesn't notice anything anyway. Nothing happens in her head, whether I do something or not. She is and always will be stupid."

How could she talk like that? I was once again stunned. I

never said anything like that again.

Recently, my father used to slip me some money, which I had 'earned'. It's hard to put into words how cold and hard-nosed this person was. Nevertheless, I accepted the money as I had nothing else. I spent almost nothing on myself, I wanted to bring some joy into my little sister's life. She didn't get any affection from my parents. They were indifferent to her, just like they were to me. But she was still so small and unfortunately also disabled. Toni needed more encouragement, much more love than I did. I would put everything on hold if it was only for her benefit. I gave her the love she never received from her parents every day. I think I can say that she saw me more as her mom than her real mother.

For her birthday, I bought her a cupcake, decorated it with a little candle and got her some play dough. My parents congratulated her in passing that morning and gave her a storybook. Toni clapped her hands and grinned. I picked up my present, lit the little candle on the muffin and sang:

"Happy birthday, happy birthday, happy birthday little Toni, happy birthday."

We blew out the little candle together. I had to help her a little with unwrapping the present, but her radiance made up for everything. We kneaded together for what seemed like an eternity. She couldn't shape figures or anything worth mentioning, but I was all the better at it. Shaping has always been my world. Antonia played with my figurines in a deep and sweet way. Unfortunately, my mother nagged me: "Where did you get the money for the present? You're not stealing, are you?"

"Mom ... I'm not stealing," I said indignantly.

"Then where did you get the money? We can't give you pocket money. I'm not stupid."
I just looked at her anxiously. What could I say?
"Don't stare at me so stupidly, where's the money from?" I still didn't answer. "Admit it, you stole the dough and the muffin," she shouted. Toni started to cry and her hand slammed into my face. I held my burning cheek and looked at her firmly. "I'm not stealing!" My sister screamed louder and louder, suddenly my father's loud voice rang out, "She got the money from me. Cecilia is no longer a baby and needs a few euros in her pocket."
"The brat gets money from you?" My mother was stunned.
"Yes, she gets it, but not much. Just a few euros as I said. And now stop fussing, you stupid cow, as if it were anything else, you're making a circus out of this." My mother looked at me in horror, then at him. Her eyes bored into his. Did she suspect something? Did she know?

My career aspirations of becoming a pediatric nurse or educator became more and more solidified. My biggest dream was to work with children. But for that I needed a secondary school certificate.
My father continued to abuse me regularly. One evening at dinner, he asked me what ideas I had for my future life.
"I want to be a children's nurse or a nursery school teacher," I announced proudly. My mother immediately laughed snidely: "You'll never manage that. You need year 10 and a good degree for that. You brat won't be able to do that." Instead of encouraging me, she put me down. But I wasn't going to be put off. My father smiled: "Good luck then." That was all he said. If you didn't have a computer at home,

you were allowed to write applications at school. I applied to three hospitals and two daycare centers. Unfortunately, I only got my documents back once with an invitation to an interview. I was very happy about that. I proudly showed the letter to my parents. My mother just waved it off dismissively, my father gave me a big look: "Now you're really growing up, my little princess. Well then, off into the big wide world." He knew full well that I still had a long way to go and that he had me under his control for as long as he wanted. Of course, I was aware that training to become a pediatric nurse would be difficult, but I wanted to do everything I could to make it. My father accompanied me to the interview, which I didn't like at all. You could see my mother's alcohol abuse and my father's too. He accompanied me with gray skin, a thick red nose, glassy eyes, unkempt and smelling unpleasant. "Dad, I'm going into this conversation alone, aren't I?"

"Yes, of course, you'll have to go through it alone. I'm only with you in case I'm needed," he smiled.

Who would need him? Why did he come at all? Because that's what fathers do?

In the end, the interview went quite well, but my performance in biology and chemistry would have to improve a lot. Everything else looked good. I made a solemn promise. The nice lady said goodbye with the words: "Then I wish you every success and we'll hear from each other." I was beaming and proud of myself. I would manage to improve my performance. Then I just had to study even harder. After the first semester of year 10, I made an appointment with the hospital's HR manager to present my half-year report and hoped I would get the apprenticeship. Unfortunately, I had only achieved a "satisfactory" in biology and chemistry and was very disheartened about this. My hopes were fading, but I still didn't want to give up. The lady looked at my certificate with a frown: "I'm very sorry, you could have sent us a copy."

"I wanted to bring you my certificate in person," I said quietly.

"But I can't decide that on my own, Cecilia. Unfortunately, I have to tell you that your grades aren't the best and we've received a lot of applications."

"Please, I'll learn as much as I can. I promise you that I will do my best." I don't remember all the things I promised. What I do know is that I had tears streaming down my face. I was so embarrassed.

"We'll let you know." With that, she said goodbye to me. It was clear to me that I wasn't going to get the apprenticeship. Why should I be lucky? I've never had that before, why now? I arrived home sad. When I told her about the conversation, my mother said: "See, I told you right away, you can't do it. Go to the supermarket, stock the shelves, then at least you'll earn a bit of money that we can put to good use." Please what? I wanted to go my own way, earn money for MYSELF, build something of my own and not stock shelves for my parents. I earn money that they can drink away? No, never. And if I don't get my dream job, then I'll do something else, but I really wanted an apprenticeship and later a job and to earn money. The main thing was to get out of this hell.

I graduated from secondary school with an overall grade of "satisfactory". Finally, school was over, I happily went

home and whirled my sister around with joy: "Yay, finally, stupid school is over." I was so infinitely happy at that moment. No more bullying. In my mind I was talking to my grandma and grandpa: 'I've made it, I've made it, now I just need an education. If I make it out of here, I'll come and visit you, for sure'.
"What are you making such a racket here?" my mother chided me.
"I've finished school - finally."
"There's a letter for you on the kitchen table. Keep it down, for fuck's sake. I've got a headache."
"A letter? For me? From whom?"
"From the hospital."
Oh dear, my heart instantly raced with fear. It was definitely a written rejection. My hands trembled as I opened the letter. I read the letter three times.

I had made it, I would get the training!!!

"Yaaaaaaaaaaaaaaaaa, yaaaaaaaaaaaaaa..." I screamed, crying and laughing all at once.
"Cecilia, that's enough now. Keep it down," my mother scolded.
"Mom, I have the training."
"So what? You're not going to get through this anyway. They're already asking a lot."
"Yes, I can do it."
My father just looked at me and didn't say a word.
That night he raped me even more brutally than usual with the words: "We have to celebrate this good news, don't we?"

Do you get used to abuse? Do you get used to pain? Definitely NO! It hurts so terribly, physically and mentally. But I never thought it would leave such a deep emotional mark on me. I always knew that everything would be fine once I left my parents' house. Unfortunately, that's not the case, you can't just shake off something so terrible. My mother's love, which I never received, still hurts me to this day. I kept asking myself why she wanted me with her? Why wasn't I allowed to stay with grandma and grandpa?

I saved the money I got from my father until I started my apprenticeship. I used it to buy a pair of jeans and two shirts. That was all I could afford. As we were a socially disadvantaged family, we got money for my training materials and for white pants. The hospital provided me with tops. I was really looking forward to my training, but at the same time I was very scared. Would the others just bully me again and ostracize me? Would I make it in the practice? What if I behaved stupidly? Or I didn't understand anything? I didn't get any motivation from home.
I bravely drove to vocational school for the first day. I was wearing my new jeans, a new shirt and had tied my long hair into a ponytail. I sat next to a nice girl in the classroom and we stood together during the breaks and talked a lot. I liked it from day one. The basics and laws of nursing, emergency situations and first aid were at the top of the timetable. I was given a great reception at the hospital. I really enjoyed everything I did. Of course, my favorite part was working with the children. However, I was often saddened by all the things the little mice could do that my sister couldn't and never would.

The horror happened in the middle of my training. I came home, completely exhausted and exhausted. My parents sat in the living room and indulged in their favorite pastime, watching TV and drinking. But today there was another binge drinker.

"Where is Antonia?" I asked the group.

"In the room, where else?", my mother spat at me. I hurried over to her. The little girl was sitting on the floor and staring ahead of her. She seemed completely distraught. I took her in my arms and cuddled her, but she pushed me away.

"What's wrong with you today? Hey sweetie, are you in pain? A full diaper? Are you hungry?" She couldn't answer me, but her absent behavior worried me. I took her in my arms and wanted to change her diaper. The little girl stiffened up. When I took her diaper off, I was almost scared to death. The little mouse was fiery red and sore between her legs. For God's sake, what had happened here? I carefully and lovingly applied cream and put a fresh diaper on her. I prepared sandwiches for us in the kitchen and took them to our room. However, the little one couldn't eat properly that day. She just stared in front of her, uninterrupted. The voices from the living room got louder and louder. I was completely alone with my sister and her distress. Suddenly I heard my name being called. The voice came from my father: "Cecilia, come here!" I obeyed and went into the living room.

"Look, that's my big daughter. She's sugar, isn't she?"

I stood there like a poodle. My mother was no longer there, she was probably already in bed. The other guy looked me up and down. His eyes made me so uncomfortable, he was literally undressing me with his eyes. "Would you like to join us for a while?" I shook my head. "No, I have to look after Toni and study."

"The little one can manage without you. Come on, you can even drink some alcohol today," my father laughed dirty.

"I'm just going to check on Toni," I replied quietly. I didn't want to join the drinking session at any price, but I was simply too afraid of getting into trouble or even getting a beating if I resisted. So I went to my sister: "Hey, sweetie, I'll be right back, sit with dad for a minute and then I'll be back, okay? You can play for a while." I gave her a doll and building blocks. I hope she stays calm, was my only thought.

Back in the living room, my father gave me a glass of wine. I absolutely detested alcohol. I never wanted to end up like my parents. Because I wanted to get it over with quickly, I downed the glass of wine too quickly. I quickly felt the effects. Everything was easier and no longer so scary. My father topped me up, but now I was more careful. I just sipped and wanted to go back to my room.

"Hey, not so fast, stay with us for a bit. You're damn pretty and cute," came from the greasy, drunk guy. Disgusting!

"No, I have to see my sister."

"Then go!" my father was angry. I left my full glass of wine and left in a hurry. My sister was lying on my mattress and had fallen asleep. I carefully laid her in her bed and wanted to finally get some rest. After washing and brushing my teeth, I fell into bed completely exhausted. The wine made me fall asleep quicker than usual.

My father woke me up in the middle of the night. He was furious: "You're coming into the living room right now." Completely sleepy, I didn't even know what was going on and trudged after him.

"If I ask you to keep us company again, then you'll do it, do you understand? What's my buddy supposed to think if you're so dismissive?" he hissed at me. Fortunately, the guy was gone.

"Dad, I had to look after Toni and I was tired too."

"Don't give me that shit, if I say you're staying with us, you're staying with us...!" He looked at me for a long time and then spoke calmly: "You know, Cecilia, you're a damn pretty thing. My buddy would love to eat you out. Of course he'll pay for it ..."

The full meaning and cruelty of my father's words only slowly filtered through to me. He wanted to sell me? I was supposed to go to bed with this guy and get money for it? The look on my face must have spoken volumes, my father immediately relented: "Hey, I was only joking, do you think I want to share you?" he laughed dirty. He came up to me, pulled me into his arms and wanted to kiss me. I turned my head away. No, not that too. He never wanted to kiss me, no matter what he did to me. He put one hand under my chin and forced me to kiss him. His slimy, disgustingly smelly tongue wandered into my mouth. His other hand kneaded my bottom. He occupied himself with me like this for an eternity until he directed me to the sofa. I had to kneel in front of the couch and stretch my bottom up. As if out of his mind, he put on a condom and penetrated me from behind. When he was that drunk, it always took a long time before it was finally over.

When he had finished, he slumped down behind me and fell asleep on the floor. I quickly pulled up my pants when I saw Antonia standing in the doorway. She didn't make a sound, just stared at me. I put her down in her crib, dragged myself into the bathroom, got some toilet paper and threw the condom into the toilet. I didn't want my mother to notice. I would be ashamed of myself. How would she react if she knew? Blame me? Beat me up? Did she perhaps even know? So many questions flashed through my head in seconds.

I was finally lying in bed, Antonia was with me and I held her close. What had she seen? Sleep would not come. How much longer was I going to put up with this? When would he finally stop?

The next day I went to vocational school despite my pain. My concentration was zero. I didn't feel like talking to the others either. Week after week, month after month went by like that. My performance got worse. I forgot far too much in practice or made mistakes. I can't count how many times I was told to pay more attention and concentrate. Nevertheless, I have to say that I was shown incredible patience. Unfortunately, I realized more and more that I was no longer up to the demands. I needed my full concentration for this training and also had to study at home. I was no longer able to do either. I could no longer concentrate on anything. I immediately forgot what I had read. In order not to drop any further, I preferred to give up. I wanted to spare myself the humiliation of being dismissed, so I finished my training from my side. Nobody tried to hold me back or encourage me to keep going. I think everyone saw and felt that I wouldn't make it. But no one asked why that was. After all, I had started with such great enthusiasm. If anyone had asked me, I wouldn't have told them anyway, so why torture myself any longer?

"There, I told you that you're far too stupid. Make sure you get a job. I'm not feeding you for free," my mother snapped at me. Dad didn't say anything.

It turned out as my mother had predicted. I found a job in the supermarket and stocked shelves. I was allowed to keep fifty euros, but I had to hand in the rest. I didn't care about anything. The only important thing in my life was my sister. I still did everything I could for her. But more and more often, the little girl was sore and just stared ahead. She didn't feel like doing anything anymore. I said to my mother: "Antonia has been so sore and red all the time lately, Mum. What is it?" But she just shrugged her shoulders: "You started training in childcare once. If you don't know, how should I know?"
"Then why don't you take her to the doctor," I asked her.
"Nonsense, a little cream on it and it will heal again."
"Not really, I already do that, but it happens again and again. It must hurt her too. She's upset and doesn't feel like doing anything."
"It's probably just a phase, it'll pass and now leave me alone with that stupid brat."

A few weeks later, I came home from work. Antonia was screaming at the top of her lungs. I could just see my mother raise her hand and hit her. She hit her bare bottom without any consideration. The little girl screamed for her life.
"Shut your stupid mouth," my mother shouted at the helpless child.
I pounced on my mother like a lioness and tore her away from Toni. I immediately took my sister in my arms and

carried her into our room. Mom stomped after us angrily. "Don't you dare interfere in my upbringing again," she yelled at me.
I didn't say anything. I looked fixedly into her eyes. I despised this woman deeply. Just like my father. I also despised him with all my heart.

A few days later I was off work and picked up my sister from her facility, I wanted to speak to her caregiver: "Have you noticed that Antonia is often so sore?"
"Yes, we did, and I told your mother to avoid acidic drinks like orange juice and to go to the doctor."
"That could be the reason?"
"It can have many causes, so I advised her to take her to the doctor."
"OK, thank you very much for your information." I said goodbye and went home with my sister. Reluctantly, my mother took Toni to the doctor and was prescribed an antibiotic ointment. It seemed to help. I was determined to help Antonia get rid of her diaper. I regularly put her on the toilet. At first she was petulant every time, grimacing, but more and more she accepted the toilet and did her business. A few months passed before the desired success was achieved. The facility Antonia went to helped a lot and my little sister no longer needed a diaper during the day. I was so proud of the little mouse. But mom was too lazy to pull together with me. When I wasn't there, she simply put a diaper on her little mouse. She didn't bother with toilet training. The result was that Toni always needed a diaper. Sad, but true. The diaper was unavoidable at night, but during the day it could have worked out great if my parents hadn't

been so terribly indifferent and lazy. Again, weeks and months went by without anything changing at home.

I dragged myself through each day with all its adversity and cruelty. However, when I bathed Antonia that evening and undressed her, she had some blood in her diaper, which she still had to wear. I was struck by lightning and stopped asking what was wrong with her. It suddenly became crystal clear to me what was happening. Dad wasn't just abusing me, he was also abusing my sister.

A small, helpless, disabled child!!!

For God's sake, no, we had to get out of here! We simply had to leave. I couldn't go alone, I wouldn't leave Antonia with these cruel people at any price. Where would I go? I had only saved a little money from the fifty euros I was allowed to keep for my work in the supermarket. I lay in bed and brooded and brooded.

Where to? Where to? Where to?

How? How? How?

The escape

My grandma and grandpa! NATURALLY, it's now or never! My grandparents lived about seventy kilometers away from us. That had to be possible. Why didn't I come up with this idea sooner? How were they both doing? Did they even want to see us? I knew nothing about them. I hadn't had any contact for so many years because I wasn't allowed to. I wouldn't have dared just go there, my mother would have gotten so upset and beaten me up, I didn't want to risk it. But now I had no other choice. Regardless of whether they wanted to see us or not, I had to put all my eggs in one basket.

It was three o'clock in the morning. I quickly packed some of my and Toni's clothes in a bag from the supermarket. I didn't have anything else. I put her cuddly toy and a small doll on top. I carefully woke the little girl and immediately held a finger in front of my lips: "Psssssst, we have to be very quiet ... We're going on a little trip, yes?" I whispered. Antonia looked at me with wide, sleepy eyes, but she remained very still. She probably sensed that something was very different here than usual. When we were dressed, I took my bag and Antonia by the hand and whispered to her: "Very quietly, mouse." If Mom or Dad caught us now, all hell would break loose here. I opened the front door as quietly as I could, but didn't close it behind us; it just stayed ajar. I was too afraid that the sound of the door closing would be heard. Finally in the hallway, down the stairs, we were outside. I made my way to the station, the next train was leaving in an hour. Luckily it was a mild night. I kept

Antonia occupied as best I could, but she was very tired and therefore grumpy. Finally our train arrived. As soon as it started, my little sister had already fallen asleep. We had to change trains once, but it was only a fifteen-minute wait.

It was at night and it was still three kilometers from the train to my grandparents. Antonia was so tired and crying. I was afraid to walk through the city in the dark. I still had some money. So I asked a nice lady at the station if she could call me a cab? I didn't have a cell phone myself.

Less than five minutes later, the car pulled up and the final sprint to grandma and grandpa's. My heart was racing with excitement. Would they open the door for us? Arrived - at last. The house stood dark in front of me. Of course, hardly anyone was awake at this time of night. We got out of the car and, holding my sister's hand, I excitedly trudged to my grandparents' front door and rang the bell with shaky fingers. Nothing moved. I tried again, again nothing. Oh no, they're not there or don't want to open the door. I rang the doorbell once more and banged on the door, tears welling up in my eyes.

"Grandma ... Grandpa ... please ... it's me ... Cecilia," I sobbed desperately. Finally, the light inside was switched on and someone came to the door. When it opened and my beloved grandma stood in front of me, I fell to my knees and cried.

"For God's sake, Cecilia? Is that really you?"

I cried and only uttered: "Grandma". Two arms lifted me to my feet again. When I looked up, I recognized my grandpa. I immediately threw myself into his arms: "Grandpa." In this wonderful moment, I didn't pay any attention to Toni. She was standing next to me, watching us with wide eyes.

I didn't notice it myself, but my grandma told me later.
"Child ... what's happened? What are you doing here? Do your parents know? Come in first."
When the door clicked shut behind us, I was overcome by an infinite sense of security.
"This is my little sister Antonia."
Grandma squatted down in front of her: "You've got a nice name." Toni clung to me, of course, she didn't know them at all.
"Toni, these are your grandma and grandpa. They're really nice and won't hurt you. I'll be with you, my little girl, I promise."
Grandma and Grandpa looked at me questioningly, looking at my sister: "She has Down's syndrome."
"We didn't know anything about the little one, that your mother had another child ... but I'll make you some tea first and then we'll have breakfast together and you can tell me what happened. Come here ..." My grandpa took me tightly in his arms and held me. His body was shaking, I could feel it immediately, but it still felt so damn good to finally be able to let go.
"You're so thin, Cecilia. Antonia is also very petite, are you eating enough?" my grandpa asked. Tears welled up in my eyes again.
"Leave her alone for now," my grandma smiled.
"Sit down in the living room and then tell us what happened."
I didn't even get that far. It came out of me straight away: "Can we stay with you? There's no way I'm going back home and I'm certainly not leaving Antonia there. Mom and Dad are alcoholics, they drink all day, we can't eat regularly

and we get beaten too. We have to get out of there,' I cried and sobbed. Toni jumped onto the couch in the living room, I followed her crying and sat down.

"Grandma ... I ... can't ... anymore."

"Child ... of course you can stay here for now. But to be honest, I don't know what we should do now."

"Me neither," I replied timidly.

"We'll think of something. If things are bad at home, we'll certainly find a solution."

The tea calmed me down a little. My grandpa had quickly made up the bed in the guest room and put a mattress on the floor so that we could sleep for the time being. Anything was fine with me, I would even have slept in a stable, as long as I was out of my parents' house and safe with my sister. Couldn't we just stay with them forever? We were told to lie down for a while, Toni fell asleep straight away and I couldn't get any rest. I was far too excited and confused. What was going to happen now? Mom would definitely bring us back to her with all her might. Maybe not me, I could decide for myself, but Antonia for sure. I couldn't let that happen under any circumstances.

After breakfast, my grandpa went into the garden with Toni so that I could talk to my grandma in peace. I told her everything, but nothing about the abuse by my father. I couldn't find the words for it and I felt so ashamed. The shame of the beatings and screams was already great enough. A child always thinks it has done something wrong and blames itself. I was no longer a small child and knew that my parents were just malicious and couldn't do anything with the word 'love'. But I still felt guilty somehow.

My grandma got quieter and quieter and looked at me in shock: "You're being beaten and not getting enough to eat?"
"Yes, even at night when Toni cries. She is disabled and sometimes cries at night. Even then, Mom can't control herself. I have to clean the apartment, do the laundry and everything else that needs doing. It was hell at school because I was constantly teased and bullied. I never had nice and nice-smelling clothes. I had to drop out of my apprenticeship because I couldn't concentrate and was completely overwhelmed. I only looked after Antonia when I was at home after school or training and now after work. Mom and Dad drink and drink ..." I was talking so fast that I was getting confused, but I wanted it all to come out. Sometimes I spoke in the past, sometimes in the present.
"Grandma, we can't go back. They'll kill us, we can't go back to you ... you."
"I don't care, Cecilia. You don't have to go back there, I'll see to that. You can stay if you want to, you're old enough. It's only with Antonia that I don't know how we're going to do it."
"The youth welfare office has been here before. They wanted to come again, but that didn't happen again."
"That's good. Then I'm sure there's a file of you."
I looked at her helplessly.
She took my hands in hers: "You know what? I'll just give them a call tomorrow."
"Toni attends a facility for disabled children. I don't even know if there's anything like that here and whether the little girl can just transfer. Would you even like to have her with you?"
She didn't say anything for a long time, it was working

inside her, then she said to me honestly: "You know, Cecilia, we ... so grandpa and I ... are a bit older and I don't know if we can manage with a disabled child. A little mouse like that needs support, doctors and much more. Didn't your parents do that?"

"Yes, they went to the normal examinations, but nothing more. Then Antonia came to this facility very late. But I practiced a lot with her and achieved a lot," I explained proudly.

I was sitting in my chair and out of nowhere I was overcome by a crying fit that was so violent I was shaking. I couldn't calm down at all. My grandpa and my sister were with us again. Antonia came to me immediately, clung to my arm and cried with me. My grandparents crouched down and put their arms around us:

"Oh dear ... oh dear ... what have you poor things had to go through? Calm down ... shh shh shh ... everything will be fine." I think I cried for an hour until I was able to compose myself. Grandpa was able to distract my sister by going to the nearest toy store and buying molds for the sandbox, then they went to the hardware store and bought play sand. My grandpa had no fear of contact with Antonia. He accepted her as she was and the little girl was happy.

When they got back, the little girl was whooping on the swing. Grandma and I went to the two of them and never, really never, have I seen such a happy Antonia. She was beaming all over her face and had very sweet, red cheeks. I quietly asked Grandpa: "Were you ashamed of her?"

"No, nonsense, why? She's so sweet and grateful. There's nothing to be ashamed of."

I fell against his chest and sobbed again: "Thank you."

Grandpa stroked my head: "Not for that. She's just as much my granddaughter as you are. Just because she's different doesn't mean we're rejecting her."
"Mom was always very snide with and to her."
A wonderful day came to an end without knowing exactly what to do next.

The next morning, I was woken by the doorbell and the incessant pounding on the door. I sat up stiffly in my bed in shock. I recognized Mum's voice: "Open up, give me my children out!"
I heard my grandparents' voices at the door:
"No, your children are staying here!"
"Give me the children - now!"
"They don't want to go home, they're not coming back."
"Then I'll call the police."
"Then do it, and get the youth welfare office on board. We know what's wrong with you and that you're beating the children. Go on, call the police!" I heard Grandpa say angrily.
That was enough. Toni had also woken up and looked at me seriously.
I raced down the stairs to the front door: "Mom?" I whispered.
"You come home with your sister immediately!" she ordered me.
"No, we're not coming home!" I replied bravely.
"How dare you contradict me? I decide where you have to be!"
I didn't say anything in response, just looked at her. Her behavior changed, she started to cry: "Please come back

home. I know things have gone wrong, but you are our children."

Now I had to cry too, but there was no way I wanted to go back. I didn't notice that Antonia was standing next to me. She watched the spectacle seriously, then suddenly she rushed towards mom. I thought she wanted to be in her arms, but no. With her arms and hands stretched out in front of her, she ran towards mom and pushed her away. A small disabled child made it with a gesture and dared to show her rejection to my mother. Children with Down's syndrome are cognitively impaired in different ways and develop much more slowly than healthy children. Emotionally, however, they are very sensitive and do what they feel at that moment. Not every child is the same, but that's how I read it and it applied to my little sister. I watched Antonia in confusion. Even mom was flabbergasted. She turned around angrily and left: "I'll be back." Puuuuuuh we had done that. Relieved, I took Antonia in my arms: "Hey, you did really well. I'm proud of you, little mouse."

The next day, I went for a walk with my sister and showed her the place. I was still very young at the time, but many memories came flooding back. However, my thoughts were not free. I was really upset because Grandma wanted to call the youth welfare office. I would have preferred everything to stay the way it was. Of course that wasn't possible, life had to go on somehow. I was so scared that Antonia would have to go back to my parents.

"The youth welfare office would like to talk to you, you have an appointment there tomorrow at fifteen. If you like, I can go with you and we can take Toni with us?"

"Oh dear ... what am I supposed to say? I'm so ashamed ..." I cried again. Terrible, I could hardly hold back my tears.
"They'll ask you questions and you just have to answer honestly. And if you want to know something, you'll get answers. It's not bad, believe me."
"What if they take Antonia away from me?"
"Let's wait and see tomorrow. Maybe the youth welfare office will find a facility for the little girl where she can continue to be supported."

I woke up in the morning with a very bad feeling, the conversation at the youth welfare office was weighing heavily on my mind. It wasn't just Grandma who went there with us, Grandpa did too. Grandma was right, there was already a file about us in which it was noted that we had already been visited by the youth welfare office.

"Can I say YOU?" the nice lady asked me.

"Yes, of course," I nodded.

"Why didn't you say anything during the home visit? Were you afraid?"

"Yes, of course I was scared. What do you think would have happened if I had been alone with Toni and my parents again?"

"But we wouldn't have let that happen. We could have taken you out of the family."

"I didn't know any of this. I was scared, I didn't know what would happen and whether I would have to be separated from my sister. I was still a child myself."

The officer thought for a long time. "I can see that something has gone wrong on the part of the youth welfare office."

She wanted to know if I had had to endure more than beatings, the conversation was now turning to child abuse. I shook my head. I would never admit that. For God's sake! Maybe then I would have to be examined, report Dad, have to testify in court - never. I didn't know if that would happen, but these thoughts flashed through my mind. I will never tell anyone what my father did to me. I don't know how much Antonia can remember. Fortunately, he didn't rape her yet. Apparently he started with her like he did with

me back then. Or is that also rape? I don't know.
"Would you like to bring your sister over sometime?"
Now we were both sitting in front of the lady. Toni held my hand very tightly.
"Hello Antonia, how are you?" The little girl didn't make a sound.
"Do you want to go back to other children and play and learn?" Toni looked at me with wide eyes.
"Hey my mouse, auntie wants to know if you want to play and learn with the other children again, but in a new school." She crossed her arms, pushed her chin forward and stuck her head up, looking at the woman. I had to laugh because it looked so cute. The attitude was like she was saying, 'Screw you all, I'm going to do what I want anyway'.
"Toni, please behave yourself."
At last she nodded.
"Great, then I'll try to get a place and call your grandparents when we take the next steps. Is that okay with you?"
"Please, don't take Toni away from me."
Sighing, the woman leaned over her desk:
"Cecilia, I want to be honest with you. Your grandparents are too old for your little sister. You're actually still too young and need to build a life for yourself. What do you think about us finding foster parents who specialize in children with Down syndrome? All three of us can talk to them and maybe you can visit your sister often or she can visit you as often as she wants?"
"Antonia can't do that. She only has me and has never been away from me. She only knows the facility and me. She won't be able to settle in there."
"But she can, believe me."

I accepted it for the time being and hoped fervently that she wouldn't find foster parents.

Over the next few weeks, we had to take Toni for a few examinations. It turned out that my sister didn't have to go to a disabled facility, but could attend a special school. With the right help and support, she would be able to do more than we had all realized until now. How could she? My parents took the first thing they were offered, the main thing was to get rid of her for a few hours.

I had a few more conversations with the youth welfare office about my sister. In one conversation, I was told that my parents had been stripped of custody. It was now in the hands of the youth welfare office for my sister. My heart raced like crazy when I heard that. They'll never put up with that. The lady was always so nice. She kept asking me about foster parents for Toni. She gave me brochures to read. I didn't know how I was going to cope with no longer having the little girl around. She wasn't that little any more, but for me she was and always will be my little girl, my little rubber toy, my little sister. I wanted to do everything I could to make sure she was okay, and if it was to be foster parents, then I had to come to terms with it somehow.

I had just been to the supermarket with Grandma, Antonia stayed with Grandpa. We were going through the shelves, packing what we needed, then all of a sudden ... THAT Smell! Sweat and alcohol. My heart started beating so hard that I couldn't take another step. My chest tightened painfully and I had trouble breathing. I slumped down, gasping for air. I was no longer aware of what was happening

around me. I just kept hearing my grandma calling my name. It wasn't long before the emergency doctor was sitting in front of me, I was given an injection and seconds later I became completely calm.
"That was a panic attack, young lady. Have you ever had anything like that before?" I shook my head cautiously.
"We'd like to take you with us and do an ECG, check you thoroughly."
"No, I'm not coming to the hospital. I'm feeling much better already."
The doctor smiled kindly at me: "That's because of the sedative I injected into you. But if you don't want to come with me, that's fine. Nevertheless, I would advise you to go to your GP and make an appointment with a psychologist. Panic attacks always have a background and you need to get to the bottom of it."
"I'll do it," I promised, without knowing how I was going to do it. As suddenly as the attack came, it was over again. We hurried, paid and drove home. My grandparents had a car, so shopping was child's play. Quite different from my parents.
Grandma excitedly told me at home what had happened to me. Grandpa looked at me thoughtfully: "Oh God, my mouse, what must have happened to you."

My grandma took me to the doctor to get a referral for a psychologist. This doctor was not nice. I gave him the documents I had received from the emergency doctor. He prescribed me a sedative, which I should always have with me for emergencies, handed me the referral for a psychologist and I was out again. On the one hand, I was quite happy to be out, but shouldn't a doctor take more time? Of course I understood that he didn't have much time, the waiting room was packed, but still. Well, that's the way it was. I had to wait six months for an appointment with a psychologist. Unbelievable. Panic attacks kept catching up with me. A smell, certain music, a bad word, the thought of being separated from my little sister - these were all triggers. They didn't happen all the time, but I had to deal with them at regular intervals. The fear of the attack was sometimes enough to trigger them. Fortunately, the tablets helped quickly every time.

I can't count how many times my grandparents asked themselves what they had done wrong in Beate's childhood. They asked themselves the question over and over again, Grandpa sometimes angrily and sadly, Grandma always cried when they asked her.

My grandpa fixed up my old room, we repainted the walls and I got new furniture. Everything fitted together nicely and smelled soooooo good. My sister also got a room, my grandparents' house wasn't exactly small. She got the furniture that I had when I was little. My grandpa didn't want to buy everything new yet because we didn't know what would happen with Antonia. Nevertheless, everything looked really smart. The furniture was still like new. But Toni crawled into my bed every night. She couldn't be alone at night. No wonder after the horror at my parents' house.

A few weeks later, I woke up to a loud roar. As if stung by a tarantula, I shot up and sat up in bed. "You're not taking

my children away from me," my mother yelled and slurred her words. My father shouted: "Get the brats out of here!" My grandparents didn't put up with them. They didn't open the door, Grandpa just shouted through the closed front door: "Get lost or I'll call the police!"
"Yeah, call the cops and you'll be charged with child abduction."
I couldn't believe how my parents were acting. Antonia started to cry with fear and I took one of my tranquillizers to prevent a panic attack, which I was sure was already on its way, as my heart was racing. How they managed to get here was a mystery to me. My grandparents didn't live around the corner. They never cared about us kids, so why were they putting on such a circus now? They shouted outside into the night for a while until a neighbor shouted back, "Quiet. We want to sleep." Finally they left.
A few days later, Mom was at the door again, it was early afternoon.
"Please, let me in, Mom, I just want to see my children." Grandma was struggling with herself, I could see that very clearly. But she was her daughter and let her in. Luckily, Mom wasn't drunk. Toni clung to my arm, I sat on the kitchen chair, my sister stood next to me and held my arm tightly.
"Don't you want to come back home?"
"No!" came from me in a firm voice. Mom got up and came towards us. Out of nowhere, my sister screamed, let go of me and jumped onto the couch. Just away from her mother. It's unbelievable to have to watch something like that, a child, a sick child, who abysmally rejected her mother. What did the little girl have to go through when I wasn't at

home? I had the worst ideas. Here the little one felt how nice it was to be loved and to be safe, everything around us was clean and we got regular, very tasty meals. It was a completely new world for my little sister.

"But how should it go on? Aren't you our children?"

"We'll find a way, Beate. Cecilia will get another education, build a life for herself, but you never helped the girl. On the contrary, she was so exhausted and broken that she had to drop out of a great education and then hand over the money she earned in her job to you. For what? For your drinking? You want to take little Antonia with you? You no longer have custody and no child can grow up in these conditions." Grandma was really talking herself into a rage. Mom started to cry: "If I come home without Antonia, Jens will go crazy. Mom ... please."

"No, the child will stay here, that's been agreed with the youth welfare office and that's how it will stay."

Once again, Mom's demeanor changed: "After all I've done for you? I was always there, always at home, looking after a disabled child and now this is the thanks I get?" she shouted into the room.

Excuse me? Did she believe what she was saying?

My grandpa said to her very calmly: "Beate, you leave our house right now and don't show your face here again."

"You're kicking me out?"

"Yes, just as you didn't want any contact with us for years, we don't want any more either. You kept Cecilia from us, who we had with us for the first few years and we loved and still love her more than anything. It was as if someone had torn our hearts out when we were no longer allowed to see her. You kept our little grandchild from us. We had no part in our little one's life. What are you trying to tell me now? Why do you want the children so badly? You never took care of them! Is it the child and care allowance for Toni that you need to drink away? Beate, we are deeply ashamed of you, our only daughter." Grandpa gasped for air, it was hard for him to talk like that: "Get out ... now!"

Mom seemed to have lost her tongue, she left without a word. This kind of behavior is very unusual for my grandparents. They are such loving people, always trying to find a solution, only wanting good things for their family. My parents managed to push my grandma and grandpa's patience to the limit. They couldn't help but throw them out the door. Hopefully they wouldn't keep turning up now.

We had been living here for three months. The phone rang. Grandma spoke kindly, thanked me and came over to me, taking my hands firmly in hers. "Cecilia, my sweetie, that was the youth welfare office. They've found a great foster family for Antonia." I immediately winced: "No, please don't," I sobbed.

"That's not all. You or we can get to know her with Toni and you can always visit her. The little one can also come to us. The foster parents are said to be very nice and already have a child with Down's syndrome with them ... Let's have a look, see how Antonia deals with it and then we'll see. The little girl needs other children. She would then go to a special school too." I was in tears. My little sister without me? That's not possible.

One of the worst days of my life began. We had to go to these foster parents. My whole being was against it. Toni always stroked my cheeks because she could feel how sad I was. I explained everything to her in detail over and over again, but it always made me cry. Grandpa was much better at that. Toni took it all in her stride. All four of us drove in the car for about a quarter of an hour and then we were already there. I liked the fact that it wasn't far away from me. We were greeted very warmly and invited in. A little girl was behind the foster mother, looking at us with a big smile. I introduced Antonia, the little girl came up to us, took Toni by the hand and pulled her along. Her name was Susanna, called Susi, she was two years older than my sister and had the same illness. We had coffee and cake. They offered us the DU right away. Their names were Stefan and Christin. My great hope was that the first good impression would not be deceptive.

"Cecilia, I would suggest that when Antonia gets here, you let her settle in first? Would that be okay with you? For a week and then you could come and visit her?"

I looked questioningly at my grandma and she nodded encouragingly. I struggled with myself: "I can't do this," I cried and ran outside, sat down on the steps outside the front door and cried. Inside, I heard the two girls laughing. What if Toni was really okay here? There was another child here for her to play with. But not seeing her for a whole week? What if she was homesick or really longed for me? Then what? Christin came and sat with me. "Look, she can play here, she goes to the special school and you can come and visit her after a week." I looked at her, crying: "What if she wants to come to me? Or cries, cries a lot or screams? Then you'll be annoyed and scold her."

"For God's sake, no. Of course we understand that the little one needs time, that's why we'd like Antonia to arrive here properly first and then we'll see what happens. I promise I'll call you if things get really bad and you'll come and see her before the week is over. But I'm sure she'll feel right at home here."

"That's true, it's very nice here. Toni will love the garden. Can I see her room?"

"Yes of course, come on, I'll show you."

The room where Toni was to live was super nice. Bright colors, white cupboards, a nice big bed with cozy bedding. In the next room, I could hear the girls running around. I went there, they were throwing pillows at each other and laughing tears. It was lovely to see Toni so happy. Today was Saturday and my sister was due to go and live with the foster family on Wednesday.

"What about mom and dad? Can they visit Toni too?" I asked my grandpa.

"Yes, they can, but only much later. Contact between the biological and foster parents should always be maintained for the benefit of the child."

"What, for the good of the child? They don't care about us at all. We're scared."

"So just don't worry about it. Who knows if they will want to visit Toni and if it is noticed that Antonia is unwell or can't cope with seeing her biological parents, action will be taken."

Wednesday - the day my sister moved house. My grandma had packed two suitcases. Yes, we now had enough clothes and they were chic because we were allowed to choose them ourselves. My heart was so heavy. I knew the foster parents were very nice, but I was still afraid that they would treat my sister badly if she cried or did something wrong.

The wounds of my childhood were omnipresent and kept reopening.

As soon as we got there, Antonia let go of my hand and ran to Susanna. She didn't even look back at me. I should have been reassured, but unfortunately I wasn't. The farewell was supposed to be short and sweet, at least that was my plan. Christin was kind enough to give me her phone number. I could call her at any time to find out how Toni was doing.

I hugged my little rubbery one tightly: "Take care, my sweetie. We'll see each other again in a week, then I'll come and visit you and soon you'll come and visit me, grandma and grandpa, right?" Tears streamed down my face. Toni wriggled out of my arms, waved to me and ran to her playmate. I wanted to tell her to take care of herself and that I loved her so much. But I didn't get the chance.

The very first night without my little sister dawned. I struggled with myself about calling Christin. No, I wanted to be strong. Toni had to be too. It must have been even worse for her than for me. The little girl was with strangers, I wasn't. I didn't sleep a minute that night. The next night, our phone rang and Christin asked me to come over because Antonia couldn't calm down. She must have had a really bad dream. Grandpa raced off with Grandma and me. When we arrived, the little girl was asleep again. Christin apologized to us a thousand times, she thought it was worse because my sister was so upset. The foster parents from the youth welfare office knew about our conditions at home.

Finally, the first week without Toni was over and I was allowed to visit her. She came up to me, gave me a big hug, stroked my cheek and said: "Cec ... " She meant me. "Say that again," I was so overwhelmed.
"Cec ...", she said, beaming at me. Then she pointed her finger at her foster parents: "istin ... efan ... Sus ... " I was moved to tears. She really seemed to be very well fostered.
"Do you like it here, my mouse?"
"Hmmm..." she beamed.
"Do you enjoy school? Are the other kids nice to you?"
"Hmhm ... Sus too."
By Sus, she meant Susanna. My little sister really blossomed. Even when we were with my grandparents for a few days, she was no longer introverted and quiet, but now her foster sister, the care of her foster parents and the support from the school did her indescribable good. It was amazing to me that she learned so quickly. Every time I visited her, she learned something new. Her language got better and better. She stopped needing diapers at night a long time ago. I had already managed that, but I was worried that she would need them again because of the unfamiliar surroundings. I calmed down a little and my tension eased.
"Hello Cecilia," Christin greeted me.
"Hello," I beamed, "I have a brand new sister," I said happily.
"Yes, the little one really seems to feel at home here and she's so sweet. You've always looked after her really well."

"Do you think so? It wasn't nice at home and it was hard to do her justice."

"I know what you had to go through. That's why you did so well under the circumstances. You were just a child yourself."

"Thank you," I breathed. "Can I play with Antonia some more?"

"Sure, go and see her."

Toni didn't want to play with me, however, she wanted to show how she engaged with Susanna. The two of them played hairdresser and then with the store. They were so sweet.

"So Toni, I have to go back to grandma and grandpa. Keep having fun here, I'll come and visit you again, OK?"

She came up to me, pressed herself tightly against me, stroked my head and cheeks and went back to her game. I started crying again, but I didn't want Toni to see them.

I lay awake at night and longed for my little sister. She was my everything. I felt like someone had ripped my heart out, even though I knew she was fine. It was so damn hard to let her go. I wanted her with me so much.

Today I had my appointment with a psychologist. She was great. I connected with her straight away. I talked about my childhood, my responsibilities and bullying at school. The conversation lasted about an hour. When I got home, my grandparents were sitting at the kitchen table looking very strange.

"Cecilia, come and sit with us."

"What happened?"

Grandma and Grandpa looked very upset and I panicked.

Grandma finally spoke:
"Your ... father ... well ... he had an accident."
"Oh..." was all I said.
"Cecilia, he died. The injuries were too severe."
So much has been going on inside me in the last few weeks, the panic attacks, my little sister's move and, above all, my childhood. Nightmares hardly let me sleep, I always felt disgusted with myself, panic attacks never stopped. All of that came back to me now. I saw my drunken father in front of me, how he was raping me, I almost physically felt the terrible pain again. I sat up straight and looked at my grandparents: "He's not my father."
"Child ... do not sin. He is not your biological father, but your stepfather and ... "
I interrupted her: "No, he's not a father and not a stepfather to me ... he ... has ... me ...", those damn tears again.
"Little mouse, what's wrong? Aren't you sad or scared or something? He's dead ... even if he wasn't good to you ... he died ..." Grandma spoke urgently, seemingly upset about the fatal accident.
"Yes, I know. No, I'm not sad and I'm not scared either. He made me ..."
"What did he do?" Grandma asked me quietly. "If you want to talk about it, then say so, if not, that's fine too. But there's still something there, we can tell."
"It started with touching, got worse and worse and then he did it properly, again and again and again. When I saw that he was also starting to touch Toni, I ran away with her and came to you. I had promised my sister from day one that I would always be there for her and that I would go through hell for her if I had to. I just couldn't do it anymore." Tears

gushed out of me, I had already crumbled a huge amount of tempo tissues. From that moment on, I no longer had a father, it was just Jens for me. Now I didn't have to worry about being reported to the police or having to go to court. He was dead, he was gone and that was a good thing. I spoke very quickly to get it over with. I just had to get it out, I couldn't deal with it myself anymore.
"And mom?"
"She didn't know," I continued to cry, even though I wasn't sure.
"Should I go now? Are you disgusted with me?"
"No, you fool. What he did to you is terrible and unforgivable, but it's not your fault. It's not your fault. On the contrary - you were right to come here."
"I'll kill him," Grandpa said angrily.
"You don't need to," I countered.

Jens was dead, my mother was constantly standing on the mat and crying for me to come to the funeral. My grandparents asked her for money, she had nothing. They gave her money, but they didn't go to the funeral service under the circumstances they had experienced, and neither did I. Paying your last respects to a child molester - unthinkable.
On the day of the funeral service, my mother came to us in the evening. She wasn't sober, but there was no alcohol for her here. I was in my room and heard loud voices. An argument. I quietly crept to the living room door and heard my grandpa say: "He abused your children, Beate. You didn't notice and if you did, you didn't do anything about it?"
"What should he have done? He loved his children. He would never do that."

That was too much for me. I went in and looked at her: "Yes, he did," I said, sobbing.

The look on her face became angry: "You brat was going for it. Do you think I didn't see you playing with your charms? You're a pretty thing." Her voice got louder and louder. I stood there like a poodle. What was she talking about? I would have seduced him...? You can't make this monstrosity up. Then something happened that I would never have expected. My grandma got up, went over to her and slapped her across the face and shouted at her: "Do you know what you're saying? Cecilia was a child, for God's sake. A child doesn't seduce her father. She suffered like an animal and she still does today. And Antonia? Did she seduce him too? A small, handicapped child, yes?"

"He didn't do anything like that," she now turned around, crying.

"Get out of my house and never show your face here again. You're dead to us," my granddad peppered her with an angry but quiet voice.

"Fuck you lying bastards," she countered, gave me a venomous look, got up and left. My whole body was shaking.

We sat wordlessly in the living room, each lost in our own thoughts, when it burst out of me: "Grandma ... Grandpa ... I ... didn't ...", I cried.

My grandma took me in her arms: "We know that, little mouse. You're not to blame at all. Still, I'd say you talk to your psychologist about it. You need to process this."

"I don't have parents anymore, Grandma. I never had any and I don't have any now. I'll never use the words mom or dad again. Never again. And please ... NEVER say princess to me. I know you've never said it before, but please don't do it either," I cried unrestrainedly.

My grandparents looked at me questioningly.

"That's what he always called me ... his little princess ... " I was suddenly seized by a choking sensation, I reached the toilet just in time and threw up violently. Grandma came after me and held my hair, then I cuddled up tightly in her arms and cried and cried.

"Little mouse, everything's fine ... Unbelievable ... unbelievable ... I can't even find the words for these abominations." My grandparents were beside themselves with horror and anger.

When we had calmed down after a few hours, Grandpa invited us: "What do you say we go to an Italian restaurant and have a really good time? Then we, especially you mouse, can take our minds off things. Are you still feeling sick? If you can't, that's fine too, of course."

"Oh yes," I said happily. "I've never been to a restaurant before."

"Never?"

"No, we didn't have any money for that and since I've been here we haven't had any time at all, there was so much to organize and so ..."

"Well then, get dressed up and let's go"

We happily took the car to the Italian restaurant. I was so excited. What was I going to eat? All kinds of spaghetti, pizzas with all the trimmings, steak? That was difficult. I decided on simple spaghetti Bolognese. Grandpa promised to take us here every now and then, including to a Greek restaurant and much more. It was so delicious, and afterwards I got a big sundae with fresh strawberries.

"Thank you, Grandpa, that was a wonderful evening." I was

infinitely grateful to my grandparents for everything they did for me, for supporting me in everything, for accepting Antonia as she was. "You are the best grandparents in the world," I beamed at them both.

"And you're the best and sweetest granddaughter in the world," laughed Grandma.

That night I woke up screaming, my grandma was sitting by my bed. "Cecilia ... Cecilia ... wake up ... you're dreaming ... " I was shaking all over, my face was wet with tears. My grandma took me in her arms and rocked me back and forth: "Shh ... shh ... shh ... mouse, it's all right, you were just dreaming." My dear grandma lay down in bed with me and stroked me until I calmed down and we fell asleep arm in arm. The next morning, Grandma and Grandpa made me promise to open up to my psychologist. Could I do that?

"Maybe you'll come with us next time? Start with that and then you can go out if you want?"

"Sure, if you want me to, I'd love to come with you."

This is how it happened. My grandmother told the psychologist that I had been abused and that Jens also started with my little sister.

"I thought something along those lines. Cecilia, would you like your grandma to stay here with you now or should she go out and wait for you?" I didn't have an answer at that moment. Should Grandma have to hear all this? Did she even want to? Under a veil of tears, I looked at Grandma: "Are you angry if you wait for me outside?"

"Oh little mouse, of course not. If you need me, just call me, okay?" I nodded.

During this time, when I told my grandparents what I had suffered, my grandma cried a lot. I immediately felt guilty and was angry with myself. I wish I hadn't said anything. Why was I burdening them with this? After a few weeks, I apologized for telling them everything and making them sad. Grandma and Grandpa said that I was right to open up and that I wasn't to blame for their sadness. Their sadness was one thing, their anger at Jens and Beate was greater.

Targeted questions from the psychologist steered me in the direction of getting the most out of me. She also advised me to write down all my thoughts and, if I wanted, my dreams too. In the next few sessions, we talked about my notes and further about my childhood. I opened up more and more. I will never forget what Jens did to me and I will never forgive him. Nor will I ever forgive him for the fact that he even attacked my helpless sister. I will also never forgive my mother for how abysmally bad and unloving she was to us children.

Through therapy, I have learned to deal with the bad things. To stop blaming myself. What I never got rid of were the nightmares and the disgust with myself.

It was my birthday. I was warmly and lovingly congratulated in the morning and there was a small parcel for me on the breakfast table. I wanted to eat something in peace first, but Grandma and Grandpa were very impatient: "Go on, unpack," they cheerfully urged me.
"Not later?"
"No, in a minute," they both laughed.
I removed the beautiful wrapping paper and almost fell off my chair. A cell phone. A very modern cell phone. "For me?" I asked, stunned.
"Yes, unpack it, don't just marvel at the little box. Why don't you take out that beautiful cell phone?"
I did, but there was another little note inside.
"Our little sunshine, all the best for your birthday. We'd like to promise you that if you want to get your driver's license, we'll pay for it. That's another present from us."
"NO! Driver's license? Me?"
"Yes, you and you can do it too."
"You guys are crazy. Thank you," tears made their way down my face, I was so overwhelmed. I had never thought about the driver's license before. Grandpa later showed and explained my cell phone to me. It rang in the afternoon, I still had no contact with anyone here, except my mother. I answered it and there stood my little sister, Susanna and her foster parents.
"Happy birthday to you. Cecilia. I'll bring the invited guests by tonight."
My grandparents stood behind me and laughed. Nothing could hold me back now. I threw myself at my sister, hugged her tightly and cried with joy and emotion. Christin said goodbye and we went inside, delicious cake was

waiting for us. The two girls gave me hair clips. In the evening at the Greek restaurant, it went better than I thought. I was worried whether the two of them knew how to eat out, especially Antonia. But I was wrong. They ate really well and we had a lot of fun. It made my heart soar to see my sister so happy and carefree.

"Thank you for a wonderful birthday, you're the best," I shouted to the group. Christin picked the children up directly from the restaurant in the evening.

"Christin, tell me, are the two girls always sweet? Do they always get along?"

She laughed: "Oh no, it's not always like that. Things can get heated, but never for long. They quickly become one heart and one soul again."

"Well, thank goodness. Thank you for letting Toni and Susi be with me."

"We'd love to, we'll never stand in your way."

Could there be any more happiness for me and Toni? Would it always be like this? Or was there going to be a low blow in the near future? I couldn't imagine that I could be happy and free from now on. At least free from violence, neglect and abuse. My soul was not free. My psyche had been stunted and injured too deeply.

Nevertheless, I had to keep going. I was fully aware that I needed a job. When I spoke to my grandparents about it, they said: "No, Cecilia, mouse, you have to do an apprenticeship. Start all over again. You can do it."

"I can forget about being a pediatric nurse. Nobody will take me on and I don't want to either. Everything would come up again."

"You don't have to, but something else. You need a decent vocational qualification. What would you like to do?" I shrugged my shoulders helplessly.
"Why don't you go to career counseling?"

I did that the very next day. They were right, I had to think about myself now and find my way. I was given very good advice and decided to become a qualified geriatric nurse. My grandparents were happy for me, but I still had no training. I wrote lots of applications on Grandpa's laptop and got three acceptances. I went to all three interviews, looked at everything and decided on a retirement home that wasn't far from us. I was already studying like crazy for my driver's license and was about to take the test. I passed the theory straight away, but I failed the practical part once.
Grandpa practiced with me over and over again on the dirt road, explaining everything to me as he drove through the city, I took a few more driving lessons and I got my license. I proudly held my driver's license in my hand. To add to the joy of the day, we drove to my sister's in the afternoon. Christin didn't mind. Grandpa took the little girl and put her in his car. Susanna wanted to come too. I didn't know what was going on, Grandpa gave me the key: "Drive a little way with the two of them. I'm coming with Grandma. Just up the road for your sister. I'm sure she'll be happy to see you driving."
"For God's sake, but not with the children. If something happens." Grandpa laughed. "Just once up the road and I'm in. It's only straight ahead."
"Yeah well, if you say so."
I drove off carefully and it went really well. "Ceci is

driving," Toni said happily. Susanna clapped her hands: "Yes, that's nice."

I still had eight weeks until my training began. Hopefully I would make it. My psychologist and my grandparents kept giving me new courage. Even Stefan and Christin motivated me. I was so afraid of rejection, lack of concentration and failure.

The students in my class were mostly nice, even if I didn't like all of them, and they didn't like me either. But on the whole it was good. I made friends with a few girls. It felt so good not to be ostracized. I really enjoyed the practice. Most of the old people were so grateful when they were helped. But many also cried because they wanted to return to their familiar surroundings, to their homes. I felt so sorry for them. Then there were those who weren't satisfied with anything and just nagged and got nasty. It was like that in life, there aren't just nice people and you have to deal with that. I was quite good at that. It was really hard at first, I took it all personally. My trainer kept telling me that I wasn't allowed to do that. These senior citizens don't mean me in particular. I had to learn to deal with it. I made friends and was now even out at night sometimes. A whole new world opened up.

I often lay in bed at night and hoped again and again that it would stay that way. I had become a happy young girl.

I didn't want a boyfriend. There was always someone who was interested in me. I blocked everything. I couldn't imagine if he wanted to kiss me, I couldn't even think about more. No, I couldn't do that. Thank you, Jens!!! You ruined my dream job and made it impossible for me to love a man.

I was coming from school and saw the blue lights from a distance, but didn't think anything of it. The closer I got, I realized that the ambulance was parked in front of our house. I immediately ran as fast as I could and raced into the house. Grandma was crying excitedly: "Grandpa's had a stroke," she sobbed. I quickly ran to him while he was being looked after. Unfortunately, he didn't see me. He was unconscious and his face was all crooked. I knew the symptoms, but not with my grandpa. Please don't!!! When he was taken away, Grandma and I drove to the hospital after him. He woke up again in the evening and recognized us, but his whole right side no longer worked.

But I encouraged Grandma: "Grandpa will go to a rehab clinic and he'll learn everything again. Grandma, he'll be fine, believe me." So I reassured her every day. I had to cry a lot myself, because there was no guarantee that Grandpa would ever get better. The doctors couldn't tell us either. Convalescence varies from patient to patient. We didn't give up hope, but it was brutally shattered. My grandpa spent eight weeks in the rehabilitation clinic, but unfortunately his condition didn't improve. He learned to do a lot of things with his left hand, but it was incredibly difficult for him.

I've never seen my grandpa cry as much as he did during that time. His speech was also very slurred, Grandma and I sometimes didn't understand him. We did everything we could for him. One evening, when I was helping him with dinner, he said in a somewhat slurred but understandable way: "Give me away. You don't have to work so hard with me."

Grandma cried, I replied: "Grandpa ... never ... we're not

giving you away, you're staying here with us. I can do it, I've learned it and I work with patients every day and now with you. You won't leave here, I promise".

"But I'm making you so much work," Grandpa cried in despair.

"No, you're not doing that. Grandpa, we love you and you're staying with us. Grandma loves you more than anything and so do I."

My sister often came to visit us and spent time with her grandpa. She had become a big, happy and openly cheerful girl. I will be grateful to her foster parents for a lifetime.

I hired a care service. I had to work a three-shift system and my grandma couldn't manage the hard work on her own. I helped her as much as I could. Caring for a seriously ill person is difficult, not only mentally but also physically.

My grandpa became weaker and weaker, he hardly had any appetite.

I had a free weekend and wanted to be there for my grandparents. Every day, I was wondering: "Why my grandpa? Why? Please don't take him away from me ... please don't. He's such a lovely person, he's always been there for his family and his wife. Please, dear fate, why? Why? Why are you doing this to us? My dear grandpa didn't hurt anyone, did he?"

That weekend, it was a Saturday evening, Grandma said to me: "Come here, mouse. We want to tell you something."

'Oh dear, what happened now?

"We signed our house over to you some time ago. When we're no longer here, you can do what you like with it ..."

"No Grandma ... please stop that ... I don't want to hear that," tears welled up.

"But Cecilia, that's very important, do you hear me? I want you to know that you won't be left destitute. We can't leave you any riches, but it will be enough for our funeral and, as I said, do what you want with the house. Sell it, build yourself something new or continue living here."
"Doesn't mom inherit the house?"
"No, that's why we signed it over to you while you were still alive. It's all yours. You can even put us outside the door," Grandma smiled at me and continued speaking quietly and slowly:
"You'll never have to worry about paying the rent." Now Grandpa was crying uncontrollably and Grandma joined in. All three of us were together and crying.
"I love you so much and I don't want you to leave me alone."
"Oh little mouse, that's life, death is part of it."
"No...", I sobbed and ran into the garden. I wanted to be alone. I would get the house? Continue living here without my grandma and grandpa? I didn't even want to think about that. I was aware that things wouldn't get any better with Grandpa, but Grandma? She was still quite fit. Why was she talking as if she was going to die soon too? Was she ill and I didn't know? No, I quickly dismissed the idea.

We spent Christmas together with Toni. On Christmas Eve, my dear grandpa was almost all tears. He could never come to terms with being so helpless, needing diapers, being fed and no longer being able to walk alone through his beloved garden. We used to take him outside in the fall, but now he could no longer do that either. He was getting weaker and weaker. We gave him all the love we could.

But the disease was stronger than us. No matter how long we fought against it, my grandpa gave up. He couldn't and didn't want to anymore. He spoke one last time, barely audible: "Cecilia ... be happy and ... don't forget me. I love you...", then he was silent. He looked as if he was asleep. But silent tears ran down his cheeks. He also told his wife that he loved her very much.

"Grandpa ... please ... stay there," I begged. I realized and felt that his life was coming to an end, but I didn't want to admit it. I have accompanied many old people to their deaths, but not my grandpa. Please don't!

Six weeks after Christmas, my grandpa fell asleep for good. Grandma held one hand and I held his other. When he was gone forever, I laid my head on his chest and cried. I stroked his face again and again: "Grandpa ... come safely to the other side ... thank you for everything ... I love you so much ..." Grandma cried loudly.

"What am I supposed to do now? I can't do without grandpa. What kind of life is that? Why is it so unfair?"

I hugged her tightly and said nothing. My grandma was so right - why was life so unfair?

After the doctor had pronounced his death, a funeral home came a few hours later to collect my beloved grandpa. I went with him to the car, I just didn't want to let him go. I cried over and over again: "Grandpa ... Grandpa ... I love you ... Grandpa!"

I was no longer a child, but I still felt like one. Like a little lost child. It was so bad that Grandma had to call a doctor. I screamed and cried. I was so sorry that my dear grandma had to see it. She was full of grief herself. I was given a sedative injection and when Grandma was asleep, I went to bed too. The injection allowed me to sleep a little. I applied for two weeks' leave, which was granted immediately.

The next morning I made some breakfast. Where was Grandma? She was always awake before me. I waited for two hours, but she never came. All of a sudden my heart started racing and I was overcome with a bad premonition. My grandma was lying in bed, sleeping peacefully. I went to her: "Grandma ... now, get up ... come on ... breakfast is ready." I couldn't get her awake. For God's sake! Grandma! I felt her pulse - nothing. Breath - nothing. I kept shaking her: "Grandma ... Grandma ... wake up! What are you doing? Please, wake up!" I begged ...

'I have to call a doctor! Yes, exactly, he'll get her awake again'. My thoughts were completely irrational. The emergency doctor finally arrived.

"My grandma doesn't wake up anymore. Just like that. My grandpa died yesterday ..."

"Calm down, please." As he spoke, he felt Grandma's pulse, listened to her heart and examined her body. Then he looked at me and shook his head: "I'm sorry, but there's nothing more I can do for your grandma."

"No ... no ... but that can't be ... what could she have died of? Bring her back ... please ..."

"Unfortunately, I can't do that. Resuscitation wouldn't work. Your grandma left us hours ago."

I shook my head in despair: "And I didn't notice anything? That ... goes ... ni ..." I couldn't continue.

"It looks like a sudden cardiac arrest. Was your grandmother suffering from heart disease?"

"Yes, she sometimes complained of a stumbling heartbeat,

but it always went away very quickly, so she never saw a doctor about it. But I don't know exactly."

"That could be the cause. The death of your grandfather, I suspect coronary heart disease in your grandmother. Without therapy, a sudden cardiac arrest can occur, which is conceivable given the psychological stress your grandma is under."

Grandpa yesterday, grandma today? Next to my sister, my very favorite? No, that's not possible. I wasn't even able to cry.

"But I can assure you that your grandma didn't suffer. She won't even have felt any pain. In such cases, the heart simply stops beating."

"How would you know that? No one can say what dying people feel."

The nice doctor looked at me: "Yes, we can say that sometimes. Your grandma looks completely peaceful, no face contorted in pain, no open mouth, no open eyes. That means she wasn't in agony. It's no consolation, but maybe you can hold on to the fact that she didn't have to suffer." He took the call to the funeral home from me, then he had to say goodbye.

The same funeral home drove up to our house. It was so cruel. Again, I went with them to the car and didn't want to let Grandma go. But I didn't scream. I was in shock. In my distress, I didn't know where to go at first. I drove to Stefan and Christin's house, as if controlled by a stranger.

"Heavens ... girl ... what's happened. You look like you've seen evil spirits."

"Yesterday ... grandpa ... went ... forever ...", I stuttered.

"Yes, we know that, you called us yourself. We are so very

sorry."

"Grandma today," I cried.

"Excuse me? Your grandma? How? ... What happened?"

"I don't know ... she was ... just ... dead in bed," I cried desperately.

"Oh my God ..." Christin hugged me tightly and gave me something to drink.

"The doctor ... said something ... about sudden cardiac arrest.

"How ... should ... I ... explain this to ... Toni?" I just stuttered around.

"Shall I help you with that?" she offered immediately.

I nodded.

My sister and I lay in each other's arms, crying. It was just us now.

That evening, I realized something: the night my grandparents told me about transferring the house to me, it was a kind of farewell to me. My grandma knew very well that she didn't want to go on living without her husband. They wanted me to be looked after and were sure that they had helped me on the right path so that I could get on with my life. But can a person influence the fact that they want to die? Or does the heart just stop? I should know because of my training, but I couldn't think clearly. I called all my relatives and friends. Everyone was stunned, no one would have thought that my grandma would follow my grandpa so quickly. The human psyche really does sometimes take strange and incomprehensible paths. Why did it have to happen to grandma of all people? Did she no longer want to be with me? Or had her heart really just stopped beating like that? Did she want to spare me having to go through everything twice? Would she rather do it once and then do it properly and be done with it? I thought about all sorts of things, but there were hardly any clear thoughts. My aunt (my grandma's sister) helped me with the preparations for the funeral service.

Of course, my grandparents had relatives and friends. They also came to visit us or we went to visit them. I didn't write much about it, but it was always very nice.

I had no more tears. I was too shocked and stunned. Like burst dams, fits of crying broke over me at the funeral service. For days.

I can't describe anything about the funeral here, it just hurts too much - still does.

It took me a long time to realize that I had lost my grandparents forever. I went to their grave every day and talked to them. Sometimes Toni accompanied me. We always made sure it was covered with fresh flowers.

I needed therapy, grief therapy. What had happened was too intense. I couldn't get through it without help.

I will never forget what my grandma and grandpa did for us.

I lived in my grandparents' house for a few more months, I wanted to make it, but unfortunately I couldn't. Everything reminded me of grandma and grandpa. The garden, the smell, the kitchen, their pots in which they cooked such delicious food. The cups they used to drink their coffee in every morning. So I made up my mind to sell everything and look for something new in the town a few kilometers away, where I worked and Toni lived. Something small with a garden. It was quickly found. My grandparents' house was big and so was the plot. What I bought now was a lot smaller, but beautifully situated on the outskirts of the city and freshly renovated. I even had money left over after the purchase and was able to buy new furniture. I continued to drive grandpa's car. I found it very difficult at first, but I got used to it. Even my job, working with the elderly, was incredibly difficult for me. Everything reminded me of my beloved grandparents.

The death of her parents hit Beate very hard. She called me every day and cried. But I didn't want to talk to her at all. I told her that too. Nevertheless, she wouldn't leave me alone for a day. At some point, I stopped answering the phone and we broke off contact again. Almost a year later, I received a call from a nursing home to say that Beate had been admitted there. She was suffering from severe cirrhosis of the liver and the doctors didn't give her much time left. She wanted to see me again. When the phone call was over, I fell onto the chair. Why did she want to see me? Can't this woman just leave me alone at last?

Today I am very grateful that my grandparents didn't have to witness the end of Beate's life. I'm sure they wouldn't have been able to cope with that, or only with great difficulty. After all, she was their only daughter. What went wrong back then that Beate became such a person? Was it my grandparents' fault? I can't imagine that, as sweet as they were. My explanation is that they spoiled their daughter completely, she didn't want for anything. That can also be a mistake in parenting, but grandma and grandpa certainly always meant well and took every stone out of her way. Apparently Beate thought that things would always go on like this and took several wrong turns in life, which is how she ended up where she was. But why couldn't she give love? I think she was still far too young and immature for a child and her disabled daughter rejected her because she wasn't healthy. I have these explanations for myself and I can deal with them.

Beate

Did I want to visit Beate? Not really, but I forced myself to. I wanted answers.

When I saw her, I was scared to death. She was a shadow of her former self, her skin was yellow, there was hardly any hair left on her head and she smelled terrible. Her belly was so bloated it looked like she was pregnant. She cried when she saw me.

I didn't hug Beate, even though she held out her arms. Now all of a sudden? She must have been afraid of dying, but I still couldn't give her any closeness. Our relationship was destroyed. She broke it and shouted it down.

"Cecilia ... please ..."

"Beate ... I wish you ..." she immediately interrupted me.

"Still mom to you."

I didn't say anything for a long time, just looked at her.

"No ... I ... don't have a mother. Beate, I hope that you will find peace. I also wish you that you will no longer be in pain."

"Why don't you call me mom anymore? Of course you have a mother, me..." she burst into tears.

"No, you're not my mother. I didn't get any love and security from you. I had that with grandma and grandpa until you tore me out of there. From that day on, I lived in hell. You didn't even protect me from Jens, on the contrary, you claimed I had seduced him? So you knew? Tell me - did you know? Me, a little girl? Did you only have a spark of love for your other little daughter? No, not even that." I paused for a moment. I actually wanted answers, but I got everything off my chest. My heart was racing to the limit.

"What was I to you? Babysitter, cleaning lady, your husband's mistress? Doormat? Something you could punch? Exactly, I was all that to you, but never your daughter. You and that sick guy from Jens took everything from me and ruined it. Grandma and Grandpa painstakingly put my individual parts back together with me and made me what I am today. I will be eternally grateful to them for that. I am a happy young woman and have a great job. Antonia has become a happy girl who is not as disabled as you thought. You would be amazed at what she can do and how she masters her life. Sure, she needs support, but she manages a lot on her own." Now I was crying. I didn't want her to see any more of my tears, I couldn't help it. Everything came flooding back at that moment.

Suddenly she said, "Yes, I knew it, but what was I supposed to do?"

Excuse me? I was stunned. It was a long time before I could continue, I was so shocked.

"Go! Take your children and go! How can you accept your daughters being abused? You really are..." I didn't want to say what I was thinking.

"But I wouldn't have been able to cope with you alone," she tried to defend herself.

"Of course you would be. I've done most of it. I would have continued to do that. I would have given everything just to finally be free and not be afraid of pain and abuse. Although ... I was also incredibly afraid of you, of your beatings, your unkindness and your screaming."

But I wasn't finished yet, there was still one thing on my mind, because I wanted to continue living in peace.

"I will never be able to forget what you did to me. Never! But you should be able to go in peace. That's why I want to tell you that I might be able to forgive you one day, but I can't promise it. But I will never forget.
When the time comes, let go of everything and slide over to the other side. That's all I can give you, Beate."
My mother cried. "Please, call me mom, Cecilia ... please."
I struggled with myself, I felt sorry for her somehow. I pulled myself together and just said goodbye: "Bye, mom."
I left with these words. A week later, Beate fell asleep. I was glad that I was with her again and could tell her about my ordeal. When I talk about her, I still only talk about Beate. I only said "Mama" to her one last time to do her a favor before she died.
I didn't go to her funeral service either. That must sound very harsh now. Had I become cold and emotionless? No, definitely not. I am very compassionate and emphatic, but this woman did too much to me and didn't protect me in any way. It was not possible for me to accompany her on her last journey. She was buried with Jens. I paid for it, that was all I did for her.
When I told my sister that Beate had died, Toni didn't say anything at first, then just said, "Good."
"You're my mom," Toni once said to me a few weeks later. That was the nicest compliment she could have paid me.

My little mouse and I live our lives with all the beauties of life, but also with the adversities that it can bring. We cope with everything, Stefan and Christin, my family (grandpa and grandma's friends and relatives) are always by our side.

I live in my chic but small house, which I owe to my grandparents. My sister works in a sheltered workshop and lives in an assisted living group. We are always in contact with Stefan and Christin, Susanna works in the same facility as Toni. I think the two of them are kindred spirits. We all visit each other regularly.

A long friendship has developed between me and a colleague at work. She is always there for me, just as I am for her.

There is a young man who shows great interest in me. Unfortunately, I have to say that I'm still not ready to enter into a relationship. But you should never say 'never'. Time will tell.

I will NEVER forget what my grandparents did for us. It was only because of them that my sister and I found the right path in life.

Cecilia says:

My dearest grandma, my dearest grandpa,

I wish so much that you are doing well, wherever you are now. Be cheerful and happy together again. Antonia and I are doing very well, and we only have you to thank for that. You will always be a part of our lives, even if only in our thoughts. But we are very, very close to you.

We will always carry you in our hearts.
We love you infinitely.

Antonia, my sibling, my little rubber band,

I love you more than my life.
If you need me, I'm always there for you.

Thank you dear Martina Woknitz

for your compassion and patience for my fate. I will never forget your commitment (you know what I mean).
I wish you continued success in your work, which I find so incredibly important.

Thanks also to the author

Dear Cecilia, I thank you from the bottom of my heart for your trust and your strength to talk so openly about your terrible childhood and youth.
Thank you for letting me write your story.
I wish you everything that one can wish a person. Stay strong, little one. I also hope for the best for your sister and wish the little mouse luck in everything she does and lots of joy in her life.

My darling, I would like to thank you for your patience. When I wrote down this terrible story in tears, you didn't hinder me, you picked me up. You were and are always there for me.
THANK YOU for that.

Dear Ms. Daniela Behr, a special thank you to you.
Thank you for letting me write Cecilia's story.
Thank you also for giving me so much courage.

Martina Woknitz

Read more from Martina Woknitz with DeBehr

Little Martina's childhood is marked by abuse and violence from very beginning. She is just five years old when her father abuses her for the first time. When the young child turns to her mother for help, she beats her daughter for her alleged lies. The father abuses her over the next few years and becomes increasingly brutal. It takes a long time for the now young woman to free herself. But then she enters a new hell: her partner brutally and unscrupulously tyrannizes her and their child ... A harrowing factual novel that wants to help other victims to take courage, to come to terms with what they have experienced, to rise up against their tormentors, to realize that it is not the victims who are to blame, but the perpetrators - and to finally break out of their fate.
198 pages paperback, 10.95€, ISBN: 9783957534989

Martina Woknitz
In der Ehehölle gibt es keine Wolke 7
Mein Leben an der Seite eines Monsters
AUTOBIOGRAFISCHER ROMAN

When I held my newborn daughter in my arms, I promised to protect her from all evil. But evil lived with us under one roof. I had moved out of my horrible parental home to live with my boyfriend in the middle of the night, unaware that I was slipping from one hell to the next. My childhood was marked by humiliation, beatings and sexual abuse. My marriage was now dominated by physical and psychological violence, brutality and rape. Michael was a great man when I met him. He was very goodlooking and we loved each other madly. But the façade crumbled. My husband became more and more brutal and showed sadistic traits. despondently endured all kinds of violence. I only escaped this hell after 20 years. I almost didn't survive. THE AUTOBIOGRAPHY OF A BATTERED WOMAN WHO ONLY FOUND THE COURAGE TO SAVE HERSELF ALMOST TOO LATE.

142 pages paperback, 10.95€, ISBN: 9783957535085

"Mom, I have to tell you something." Her mother looked at her, annoyed, and waited. Since the little child had fallen silent, she barked at the girl: "Yes, what now?" "Dad ... Dad ... has ... tonight ..." Martina's childhood and youth are characterized by sexual abuse by her father and beatings by her parents. She is abandoned from an early age. At the age of 19, she meets her future husband and moves in with him. But this man is not the loving and charming partner she had dreamed of. He turns out to be a violent bully and alcoholic who beats and rapes the young woman. Fleeing to a women's refuge offers no lasting protection, because her husband is on Martina's trail. She soon finds herself in mortal danger. Even as a small child, the author was the victim of constant sexual assault by her father; her husband turned out to be a sadistic rapist and wife-beater. She incorporates her experiences into this novel.

182 pages paperback, 10.95€, ISBN: 9783957535382

Our son's girlfriend had gone into labor in the seventh month! We arrived at the hospital in a hurry. My son was standing in front of us, his shoulders drooping. The doctor had already filled us in. "You're both taking drugs and drinking alcohol? Both of you? Saskia is PREGNANT ...!!!" I had already heard enough of the subsequent assurances that I wanted to stop. Anna's son Lucas is addicted to drugs and alcohol. Even when he becomes a father, his behavior doesn't change. Aggression, violence, theft and lies, including to his mother, who tries in vain to help him, dominate his everyday life. He calls her a shitty mother. Lucas continues to plummet. And Anna is advised to let him go in order to protect herself. But how could a mother let go of her child? And what will become of the little granddaughter?

198 pages paperback, 10.95€, ISBN: 9783957536822

Jenny grows up in an unimaginably cruel home. Beaten and humiliated by her mother, severely sexually abused and mistreated by her father since kindergarten age, the little girl ekes out her terrible existence. When her mother separates from the tyrant after years of martyrdom, everything seems to get better.
But instead of finally protecting her child, Jenny's mother exposes her to new cruelties.
After years of horror, the girl ends up in Frankfurt's Bahnhofsviertel district. Alcohol, drugs and the perverse desires of the customers of the baby prostitute now determine her everyday life. Soon her life is hanging by a thread. The true story of a lost child.
182 pages paperback, 11.95€, ISBN: 9783957538383

My father kicked her with all his might. Mom screamed: "Stop it!" "Then put something proper on the table for once, you stupid cow." He kicked her again and again until Mum was lying on the floor, completely exhausted and crying. Why didn't she leave with us? Why didn't she at least protect us, her two little sons? How could she allow what this monster did to us and what would drive my brother to suicide? Paul grew up with his two-year-old brother Jan in an unbelievably cruel family home. The children are defencelessly exposed to the beatings of their choleric father and an inactive mother. The father soon begins to abuse his sons and rape them severely. Jan breaks apart as a result. Paul, on the other hand, ends up in a spiral of violence, drugs and alcohol. He fears becoming like his father. But then Jana enters his life. The true, gruesome biography of an abused boy who becomes an abuser himself.

236 pages paperback, 11.95€, ISBN: 9783957538963

I don't remember when I started to develop a fear of my father. I didn't go to school yet. I think I was five years old... From her earliest childhood, Elisa is at the mercy of her father's anger. On the outside, he plays the perfect husband and dad. But Elisa and her mother suffer from his brutality, are tortured and humiliated. One day, he begins to rape the little girl. The child silently endures the abuse until she can take no more and confides in her mother. She promises to protect her daughter from now on. But instead she takes the most terrible path a mother can take - she takes her own life and leaves her child abandoned and at her mercy. Now Elisa is alone with a monster... A harrowing factual novel that aims to help victims take courage, come to terms with what they have experienced, rise up against their tormentors and realize that it is not they who are to blame, but the perpetrators.

Paperback with 242 pages, price: 12.95€, ISBN: 9783987270017

Printed in Great Britain
by Amazon